FROM A HIDDEN STREAM
THE NATURAL SPIRITUAL AUTHORITY OF WOMAN

A Primer for the Future of Humanity

by
Vajra Ma

FROM A HIDDEN STREAM

The Natural Spiritual Authority of Woman

A Primer for the Future of Humanity

ISBN: 978-1-4507-3384-7

Third Edition 2013 / 2016

© 2010-2013 by Vajra Ma
© 2013-2016 by Shakti Moon Publishing
a project of the Shakt i Moon Foundation

VajraMa@Shakti-Moon.com

All Rights Reserved

If you wish to quote or extract any material from this publication, except brief sections for review, please do so only with explicit written permission from the author.

Cover design and typesetting by Wolfgang Nebmaier

dedicated to the

ANCIENT
   FUTURE
      SISTERHOOD

FROM A HIDDEN STREAM
THE NATURAL SPIRITUAL AUTHORITY OF WOMAN

Hidden just beneath the surface of our experience there flows a living stream, untainted by the poisons of fear, ignorance and greed. Though deliberately erased from view for the few millennia called history, this stream cannot really be eradicated because it is the source of everything, often also named the animating force of the cosmos. To those who let themselves feel it, this hidden stream is a visceral reality. And to those who shed the blinders of materialistic indoctrination it is visible in everything. The tantrics of yogic science call it "spanda". In the ancient Indian tradition of the Divine Mother, it is called "Shakti" the Feminine power. It is the oldest spiritual lineage on Earth, humanity's more than 200,000 years of universal reverence for the source of life: The Great Cosmic Mother.

Though forgotten for millennia, deliberately erased from our memories and our history from generation to generation, this stream exists. Though hidden, it cannot be removed because it is reality. Though hidden, it is not far. We have only to turn our gaze inward, focus and release ourselves into this stream.

This primer is an invitation to enter this hidden stream, let it flow through us and eventually from us. We can drink from this source directly, receive the wisdom directly, wisdom untainted, uncodified, wisdom natural and alive. It is the living stream of female wisdom. The same cosmic power and wisdom that empowers women's bodies to gestate, birth and nurture life.

I was 35 years old before the idea of a Mother Creator was introduced to me, a concept which seemed strange to me at first, but once I was over the inertia of my conditioning, it made much more sense than its widespread and accepted reversal. And, once given

The Basis of Woman's Natural Spiritual Authority

the Rosetta Stone by Mary Daly and many other feminist authors, to decipher the reversal which had demonized the Great Mother, I proceeded to reverse the reversal in my own consciousness. I opened Pandora's Box! True to the Great Reversal[1] this box was not filled with curses, dangers and evils, as threatened in the patriarchal distortion of Pandora's original story, but abundant with the rich and varied gifts of a loving Mother Creator. Pandora literally means "giver of all gifts". Pandora's Box is rich with the legacy of Woman's Natural Spiritual Authority.

"With Woman's .. what!?"

If that is what you are thinking, then you, as I once did - along with a majority of the human race - do not know that Woman once held spiritual authority in the world, let alone that we came by it "naturally".

Like most average Westerners, I grew up in a world where the Tree of Knowledge in the Garden of Eden, was forbidden. The ancient symbols of the Great Mother's serpentine life force rising through the human body, the Tree of Life, had been reversed into symbols of evil. Especially the female body which is the Tree of Life *par excellence*, which is literally "carnal knowledge", was equated with the source of everything that ails humanity. However, this demonization or, at best, misogyny of Woman, was not at all part of the original teachings of Jesus, nor Mohammed or Buddha. Yet the patriarchal institutions built on their names regressed into misogyny and permeated western Judeo-Christian, as well as Islamic, Hindu, Buddhist and most other cultures with that misogyny, which now extends globally into all systems based on these institutions and supported by them.

---

[1] Mary Daly's term.

The Physical and the Spiritual Are Not Separate

I had been walking the path of modern Goddess spirituality, a movement that began in the late 1960's, for nearly twenty years before this particular string of words came to my mind: *"woman's natural spiritual authority"*. Though women's spiritual authority is a re-claiming that is central to the modern Goddess and women's spirituality movement, I had never read or heard this exact string of words before. It came to me as I was preparing a lecture for The Goddess Temple of Orange County, founded by Ava Park. Years earlier, I had encountered feminist author Vicki Noble's term "female spiritual authority" and probably tucked it away in a corner of my mind. But the word "natural" had not been connected to the context of spiritual authority, and it suddenly catalyzed a cascade of connections and realizations that reverberated in my body and has continued to multiply and expand even as I write this book.

We are embedded in a world view constructed largely on the premise of overcoming reality, a world view that inverts the preceding more than 200,000 years[2] of Woman's natural spiritual authority. This reversed world view declares man as the head of the female and the female as the bringer of death and sin into the world. And it uses myths to prove and enforce its point.

THE BASIS OF WOMAN'S NATURAL SPIRITUAL AUTHORITY

Though my personal spiritual path is Goddess oriented, Woman's natural spiritual authority can operate and has operated both within patriarchal religion and outside a religious context altogether. Some of the women's stories shared in this primer will illustrate this.

---

[2] The oldest recorded Goddess figurine, the Acheulian-culture Berekhat Ram figurine, was found at the Golan Heights in 1981 by archaeologist N. Goren-Inbar of the Hebrew University of Jerusalem. It is dated between 230,000-700,000 BCE.

The Matrix of Woman's Natural Spiritual Authority

The dynamics of Woman's natural spiritual authority are based in nature, in reality, and they are universal to Woman regardless of belief systems and societal constructs. Thus the word natural. And herein lies its tremendous power to "save the world". The reader can rest assured that seeing validity in the information presented here does not require a conversion to any particular spiritual path or viewpoint. We do not need to construct new governments, institutions, bureaucracies, non-profit organizations, belief systems, cultures and religious dogma, nor do we need to destroy the old. We merely need to wake up to reality. The rest will follow. Right action arises with stunning alacrity and accuracy when reality is the inspiration.

THE PHYSICAL AND THE SPIRITUAL ARE NOT SEPARATE

In reality we do not experience a split between the physical and the spiritual, between natural vs. divine. Neither reality nor human experience provide for such a dichotomy. It arises only with the advent of patriarchal religions which are based on the artificial doctrine of separation. In fact, far from being separate, it is from the nature of the female body, which encompasses Woman's power to create life, that a cascade of inseparable emotional, physical, mental and spiritual dynamics unfolds, naturally and spherically. This is the basis of Woman's Natural Spiritual Authority.

THE MATRIX OF WOMAN'S NATURAL SPIRITUAL AUTHORITY

This primer will provide insights into the reality that, evolutionarily and historically, women are the creators of humanity. This goes beyond the mere physical but encompasses the cultural, artistic, and, most of all, the spiritual[3]. For millennia, Woman was the

---

[3] . It is not within the framework of this primer to provide the full scope of abundant historical, archaeological and anthropological evidence to this

spiritual authority of humanity. This is historical fact. It is only in the past 6,000 or so years of recent humanity, that myth and propaganda has attempted to turn this upside down and backwards.

We will see that the scope of riches that evolved from Woman as the Creator of humanity is a natural extension of Woman's relational power in birthing, protecting, sustaining, teaching and guiding her children, humanity. Humanity is Her child and as she holds her child in her arms she is the creator and first teacher of humanity. This includes women who do not have physical children. And as there is no true separation between the spiritual, the cultural and the artistic, that teaching embraces all.

We will see the historic reality of Woman's natural spiritual authority. We will recognize women as the original shamans, as priestesses, midwives, healers, curanderos, devadasis, the Mothers, wise women (witches), holy women, tantrikas, tribal queens and leaders.

As the image unfolds of Natural Spiritual Authority, we will discover how it differs from the imposed and enforced dogmas and doctrines of the patriarchal paradigm. Because what grows naturally based in Woman's natural spiritual authority is love, protection, nurturance and guidance of the life she has created, not only for the physical children she has created in her body, but for all life, for her own Motherhood is embedded in a vaster Motherhood of Earth and the cosmic womb.

'MOTHER MIND'

Men too can participate in this Motherhood by opening and connecting to all around them in a direct, sensate way, unfiltered by dogma or conditioning, by recognizing that this connection is

---

effect, however, references for this evidence are provided in the 'Suggested Reading' list in the back of this book).

The Matrix of Woman's Natural Spiritual Authority

more easily accessed by women, and by revering and respecting women in their spherical, holistic sensual awareness. This leads to a recognition and realization that this is not other than spirituality but central to it. As men do this they, too, open to what Zulu healer Credo Mutwa calls Mother Mind, "that part of human consciousness that feels what is happening in the world."

When we look at reality, the world around us, we see that what authors life has authority in relation to that life and this authority is inseparable from responsibility. Authority exists in *relation to*, not by might or force over. We will see how relationship is the determining factor in *natural,* that is, authentic authority. This authorship emerges from power, not force, from relationship and responsibility, the *'power with'*, and not from violence and domination, the *'power over'*.[4]

By now, Motherhood must be obvious as the central and permeating dynamic in Woman's natural spiritual authority. Natural authority is inseparable from reverence for life. From love. The quintessential embodiment of this reality is motherhood. This is Motherhood with a capital M, encompassing both the highly personal experience of being a mother and the transpersonal experience of the supreme spiritual principle of love intrinsic to Motherhood.

Ammachi, the "hugging saint of India" who is recognized as an embodiment of the Divine Mother describes the universal essence of Motherhood:

Ammachi on Universal Motherhood

"Anyone, woman or man who has the courage to overcome the limitations of the mind can attain the state of universal motherhood. The principle of motherhood is as vast and powerful as

---

[4] Feminist author, ritualist and activist Starhawk coined the terms 'power over' and 'power with'.

the universe. With the power of motherhood within her, a woman can influence the entire world. The love of awakened motherhood is a love and compassion felt not only towards one's own children, but towards all people, animals and plants, rocks and rivers, a love extended to all of nature, all beings. Indeed, to a woman in whom the state of true motherhood has awakened, all creatures are her children. This love, this motherhood, is Divine Love and that is God."[5]

Nothing embodies and exemplifies the interweaving of power and responsibility more aptly and completely than the icon of Mother and Child. By exploring this timeless sacred symbol, we will retrieve its meaning, the power of Motherhood, and go about restoring it from the ravages of dismemberment. This dismemberment severed motherhood from female sexuality (as in the Catholic church's version of Mary giving birth as a physical virgin) and excluded values of Motherhood from cultural and political leadership.

As we view what has unfolded from the reality of the female body, we will also discover this is by far no limiting essentialism or biological determinism but rather places Woman in an expansive context of natural and therefore undeniable powers. The fear of these undeniable powers is the reason why patriarchy has vilified and demonized the female body and flesh in general. On the other hand, to further usurp natural motherly authority, the male is glorified. This creates a contrived male authority, which is a reversal of reality and can only be kept in place through the mythology of male motherhood. This mythology often includes the recurring theme of dismemberment of the original Creatrix by the god-hero who then boasts about "his" creation. We will see how this pervasive dynamic

---

[5] http://www.amritapuri.org/amma/un2002/awaken3.php An Address given by Mata Amritanandamayi Devi on the occasion of A Global Peace Initiative Of Women Religious And Spiritual Leaders, Palais des Nations, UN, Geneva, 7 October 2002.

of dismemberment plays out in the world today. Thus, our investigation will expose just how profoundly the spiritual is political.

The view through the lens of "reversing the reversal" will reveal how the iconography of woman's natural spiritual authority has been co-opted and distorted and how we can decipher the original meaning through the distorted vestiges. Recognizing the original meaning and intent of familiar images -- New York harbor's Statue of Liberty, for instance -- gives us a sense of how woman's natural spiritual authority is not "other" to us but often closer than we may have imagined,

THE RELEVANCE OF 'REVERSING THE REVERSAL'

This series of discoveries and their consequences matter because the dismemberment of Woman from her natural spiritual authority has played out over the centuries in a cascade of violence, greed and suffering, and has brought humanity to the abyss of self-destruction. The issue of restoring woman's natural spiritual authority goes to the very root of what ails the world, quite the opposite of the dogma that blames her for it, and of the dominant myth that drives us apart from each other, 'justifies' violence, destruction, greed, pollution, rape, and the privilege of some at the expense of most.

We will see how woman's natural spiritual authority is not peripheral or marginal to the crucial issues of the age, but central to solving the ills and relieving the suffering in our world. Woman's Natural Spiritual Authority is re-emerging as *The Key To Planetary Peace*. It is the key to bringing humanity back into right relationship with Earth and each other. The stories of modern women, acting in extraordinary ways "out-of-the-box" will indisputably illustrate this.

The Relevance of 'Reversing the Reversal'

Actions by Contemporary Women and by Modern Women from the Past

These stories will show how one woman's "silly dream" was the beginning of the end of a brutal civil war; how one woman of the lowest "untouchable" caste in India donned a hot pink sari and carried a big stick demanding that men stop beating their wives and now leads tens of thousands of Indian women in a successful crusade for justice; and how one woman followed the simple wisdom "If you start with your relations, then everything will unfold naturally" and now thirteen indigenous grandmothers fulfill a centuries old prophecy travelling the globe in behalf of peace.

Each of these Grandmothers acts from her natural spiritual authority, whether she would call it that or not, for "Woman's natural spiritual authority" is not an invention, it is a phrase that names an actual phenomenon arising from a matrix of factors. We will discover the common elements of woman's natural spiritual authority that are operating in all these women's actions, the instinctual protection by mothers of their children, their self-referenced trust in their deepest feelings, motherly common sense action in service to life. No bureaucratic "red tape".

We will also take a look at a few women from the past, such as the Catholic nun who chastised princes and popes and got away with it, or the author who decried the misogynist underpinnings of the 14th century European society in which she lived.

We can draw inspiration from women past and present to step outside the box of patriarchal confinement. We can drink and nourish ourselves from the hidden stream of inner feminine wisdom. Each of us can refer to our own experiences and allow ourselves to remember, to feel what we, personally, once wanted to do, what we can do now, what impulses and desires are rooted in natural spiritual authority. Once Woman's natural spiritual authority is named, a foundation is set from which to act.

The Matrix of Woman's Natural Spiritual Authority

Woman's Body as Evolutionary and as 'Calibrator of Reality'

We will investigate how the following fundamental dynamics of Woman's body and psyche unfold naturally into a comprehensive and therefore spiritual authority:

the womb as physical creator,
the womb as spiritual source
the female body and psyche in totality:
- as matrix of Woman's spherical and holistic sensual awareness,
- as calibrator of reality.

The womb as physical creator, the conduit of our descendants, makes it the **portal of the future.** It is a spiritual creator in that it is the dreaming and visioning source as during menses Woman's perception naturally extends beyond the apparent boundaries of time and space as confined by our rudimentary five senses. The womb is therefore a portal of both the past and the future, of Ancestral wisdom[6] and of inspired vision for the future, both of which are more easily accessed when Woman is bleeding.

This access to wisdom and inspiration, related to hormonal and chemical changes, then continues on a more steady, continual basis after women complete their many years of blood cycles and become 'grand' mothers. The womb maintains what I call the Ancient Future Sisterhood.

In its totality, Woman's body with its spherical, holistic, sensual awareness and integrated sexuality represents a matrix that is a supremely subtle and sophisticated calibrator of reality. It operates in alignment with the reality that the physical is not separate from the spiritual and has led the evolutionary way for humanity.

---

[6] "Ancestor" with a capital A is not limited only to human predecessors, but includes our genetic, evolutionary heritage.

THE MATRIX AND THE ONLY ONE

There is no such word as 'patrix', and that is for a good reason.. Woman, womb, life, and the cosmos are the only plausible and legitimate references for using the word 'matrix'. Matrix is defined *as a situation or surrounding substance within which something originates, develops, or is contained; the womb; and as a binding substance.*[7]

Woman's natural spiritual authority is based in reality. There almost arises the question if that authority should indeed be referred to as being derived from (based in) rather than intrinsic. After all, the nature of woman, including her body, her womb, her psyche, female modes of functioning, the entirety of these facts is interrelated in a matrix. Even though the apparent lack of definition and precision in the notion of a matrix seems to contradict what is generally perceived as the nature of authority, it is this very non-linear nature, the 'lineage from within', the hidden stream, which is at the core of Natural Spiritual Authority.

AUTHORITY VS. APPROVAL

Woman does not need approval or to get anyone to understand or agree, does not need to convince anyone, all of which are traps that tend to stop women from claiming their natural spiritual authority. Natural spiritual authority does not need that. And in a framework of natural spiritual authority, a woman is not deterred when approval or "understanding" is withheld.

A poignant example of this is found in an article by Krista Bremer in the February 2008 issue of The Sun, where she describes the process that led to her allowing her son be circumcised. She had tried to convince her husband, who was Muslim culturally, but not religiously (he even argued with his family for the rights of his sisters), why it was wrong to do it. She tried to have him approve of

---

[7] American Heritage Dictionary, Second College Edition, 1982.

The Matrix of Woman's Natural Spiritual Authority

her feeling against circumcision. After a long and painful struggle, she finally ran out of plausible arguments.

The one thing she did not do is say "no".

If she had said something to the effect "This child came out of my body and his body will remain as it is created." she would have acted from natural spiritual authority.

Natural spiritual authority trusts and relies upon the knowing about life and about protecting life that is often denigrated as "mere instinct" rather than acknowledged in its true scope. Woman must step back into that natural spiritual authority -- take that responsibility and take that risk -- because, ultimately, there is no survivable alternative. Humanity needs this from women in order to survive!

The good news is that women can wake up to that comprehension of themselves in an instant because the natural spiritual authority is there, just under the surface in a hidden stream. And it must be there: It is reality.

Even though it has been hidden, deliberately erased from history, there remains in many people's consciousness the memory and the imprint of an original awe for Woman, and with it comes a sense of how Woman's natural spiritual authority was usurped and replaced with an imposed, ultimately world negating religious authority. This religious authority, based in fear, has had a devastating effect on the course of civilization, from daily life to governments to our treatment of Earth, body, women and her children, humanity.

Natural spiritual authority is not derived from a book, is not codified, has no rules but rather comes from deep feeling, from a totality, from relationship, from a surrender to the wholeness of life. The only book it is written in is the body, mind and heart. Wisdom, instinct, caring, love, relationship, responsibility, all these factors in the matrix of woman's natural spiritual authority cannot be reduced to a college course, a step-by-step instruction manual or a list of commandments.

Woman's natural spiritual authority is written in the body, mind and heart of men as well. When they stop the mantra of separation, really listen and feel, they will recognize it. 'Mother Mind' aligns the male with what comes naturally to the female.

To catalyze a paradigm shift from male domination to egalitarian partnership, will take a critical mass of women come to fully recognize their natural spiritual authority. Recognizing authority as coming from within rather than being contrived and imposed from without, will change our understanding of the nature of authority itself. When authority grows from a relationship to the whole, love and authority are twin sisters.

WHAT NATURAL SPIRITUAL AUTHORITY IS NOT

DOMINATION AND IMPOSITION

What Natural Spiritual Authority is not is imposed, artificial, contrived and therefore does not foster nor require a culture of coercion and violence to maintain it. Natural authority, as we will see, is embedded in relationship and responsibility. Authority in contemporary civilization operates predominantly severed from the natural relationship between creating and being responsible to that creation. It sanctions itself apparently referencing the intellectual linear mind, rather than the innate (meaning: we are born with it) feeling, knowing and relating. It comes from disconnection, rather than connection; from privilege and "rights", rather than relationship and responsibility.

The original relationship, naturally embodied in the mother-child relationship is absent in "authority" today. Most authority in modern society is divorced from responsibility and disconnected

What Natural Spiritual Authority Is Not

from relationship. Think of political 'leaders' who send young people to kill and die in war. Authority that is outside relationship and responsibility is not natural, but is a contrived, artificial, abstract imposition on the freedom of others through force, coercion or threat. Once that artificial concept of authority is established, it is shored up and enforced through laws, governments, institutions such as marriage and male-identified religion and dogma. This false authority is self-serving, it dominates for the sake of self-gain, not for the sake of serving life. It represents the direct opposite of natural in that instead of cradling us in love and nurturing it derives its 'power' from threatening to withhold love and nurturing, to take it away, essentially by threatening to deprive us of and separate us from the life-giving source.

Force Over

Since anything imposed must be kept in place by unnatural means, force and domination, rules, concepts and laws must replace the mutuality of natural relationship. To be able to do that, one must first rip the Source from Her natural, innate place and appropriate it as a commodity under the control of the artificial authority where it is used to coerce and threaten.

In this way, false authority operates divorced from life, from the body and the actual processes of birth, death and rebirth. It is based in a concept of reality, not reality itself. It is the reductionist, logical, linear mind divorced from and in dominance over the creative powers of life. As it is unnatural, it cannot last but, like a disease, is likely to destroy its host, humanity (while doing a lot of collateral damage).

We see this also in the glut of ever louder and more violent American hero action films whose previews in the movie theatre are at times almost seamlessly following an extensive high production value advertisement for the national guard or other military establishments. Instead of glorifying the first blood of a young woman, the entertainment media inundates us with glorification of violence, life-taking not life giving, the blood of death, not the blood of life. In fact the blood of life is apparently so repugnant to the modern eye that menstrual pad commercials depict menstrual blood as blue.

DISMEMBERED FROM SOURCE

Severed from the source of creativity, authoritarianism is non-creative, at best stagnant but essentially dead. It is the action of the spiritually dead trying to create more of itself: deadness. Without the self-sustaining vitality of connection to Source it must instead perpetuate itself through violence, enforcing its fatal objective with the terrorism of warfare, rape, disease, and, at its least overtly violent, creating suffering through soul numbing consumerism and wage slavery.

ABSURD REVERSAL

Such a society, intent on feeding death is the natural consequence of the usurpation of Woman's spiritual authority by a male motherhood, a mockery, frankly, as characterized by Greek mythology's Zeus giving birth from his forehead, or by the Judeo-Christian bible's male god surgically extracting a male rib to make from it a female, life-giving being. Both are literally as far removed from the reality of birth as the forehead is from womb or a dry bone from the fecund vulva.

If we step back and look at another species, we see how absurd it would be, for example, to try and create a "law" that put the male lion in charge of rearing the cubs. How would the male lion be made to take on the responsibility or the lioness to relinquish hers? Where would the male lion get the skill to raise the cubs? There probably are some rare cases documented about maternal male lions but, in general, when male lions come across a litter of cubs they will kill them in order to mate with the female and ensure the survival of their own genetic material.

WHAT IT IS

We will end up understanding all parts of the expression of Natural Spiritual Authority of Woman as a matrix, as inseparable and mutually conditioned upon one another. It bears saying again that this is not something new, something "made up". It is simply a name given to the observation of a natural matrix of factors which has been operating for millennia. A brief investigation of each word will lead to the telling discovery of how interrelated the words are in "Woman's Natural Spiritual Authority".

WOMAN

A capital "W": Woman, as opposed to "women", i.e. a number of female persons, signifies the collective consciousness and gestalt of women as a group, of life. Woman means women as a collective. Woman is neither the opposite of male nor the other half of men. Woman connotes the archetypal, universal biological, mental, emotional and historical scope of being female. It embraces all aspects of human femaleness and is infused with the broad, overarching reality of being a life-giving source. It also includes the instinctual response to danger. This is not an excessive "hysterical" overreaction but an appropriate in-the-moment response to reality. It is not a bureaucracy or set of laws nor a religious dogma or other institutionalized, deadened path, but a direct path to immediate, realistic, and commensurate response.

Woman does not exclude the assertion of spiritual authority by individual women in their lives and in society, for there is no collective without individuals, but it does so in a way that references the wholeness of life and values the collective wisdom. This was what is termed in the South African Bantu language as the spirit of "Ubuntu"—"I am what I am because of who we all are."

A clear example of the collective wisdom of Woman in operation today is related by Grandmother Bernadette Rebienot, one of the International Council of Thirteen Indigenous Grandmothers.

Natural

She attributes peace prevailing in her homeland of Gabon (Central Africa) to the fact that the government listens to the women. For centuries, Gabon women have gathered in the forest to share their visions, pray for world peace and the well-being of their people. "In Gabon," Grandmother Bernadette says," when the Grandmothers speak, the President listens. There is war all around us, but there is no war in Gabon." [8]

The President of Gabon did not listen to one woman only, but to the wisdom of the collective of Grandmothers who joined together, sharing their individual visions and inspirations. For when women come together in a group with a spiritual intent there is that collective consciousness, a deep mind that arises from a hidden stream, a fountain of deep wisdom that is bigger than just one individual mind and its concepts, and of a scope beyond present time and contemporary experience.

I have experienced and facilitated women in ritual and moving meditation this way since 1985. I call this the female shamanic group, the *Ancient Future Sisterhood*. Women then tap into the innate body-knowing and depths of the human heart, the heart of the Creatrix, the supreme natural spiritual authority. And when we tap into this heart we are guided by this supreme natural wisdom and spiritual authority, the Author of all life.

NATURAL

A life-giving source authors life, naturally. Authority thus is an inherent part of life-giving, of authorship. There would be no life without it. After all, authority it is not at all an artificial, abstract imposition on the freedom of others. Authorship is where life comes from.

---

[8] http://www.nativevillage.org/INTERNATIONAL COUNCIL OF THIRTEEN INDIGENOUS GR/Each GR Home Page/Bernadette Rebienot/Bernadette Rebienot Homepage.htm

What It Is

The best pattern for authority in nature is its fundamental manifestation in mother and offspring. It is not imposed and it never really ends but expands into being an integral part of the experience of life. Mothers lead their baby, cub, kid, foal or calf through the early, formative processes of life. For good reason, one of the oldest epiphanies of the Goddess is the lioness. She is an incomparable mother, protector and provider.

The lioness who creates her cubs is supremely responsible to them. She protects, guides, warns and sets limits. And these limits, warnings, and guidelines are not arbitrary or artificial, not abstract concepts separated from reality, and they are not self-serving for the insular benefit of the lioness, but are in direct, intelligent relationship to reality. The Lioness mother provides food, guards against predators and knows when to hide or run for safety or to stand and fight. The mother exercises authority over her offspring not in an ego-fest of domination, but on their behalf, *in service to them*, in natural interrelationship with them. The babies know this and their response to her authority is the very thing that enables them to survive and mature into adulthood.

The same is true for a woman and child and her responsibility to care for that child, including the responsibility for the additional human dimensions of emotional, mental and spiritual maturation. This is natural, and there is nothing as natural as this. Of herself (in a woman and child supporting culture), no mother would relinquish or neglect her child, let alone let it be whisked away to undergo any number of unnecessary, alienating and traumatizing procedures. Naturally, a mother nurtures, protects, teaches. As such, woman has authority over that child, a natural authority born of her responsibility for the life of that child. There is no separation. There is no: I want a child. I'm going to get myself a child. Then I am going to do something with and to it. And then I'm going to go on with my life. Woman is mother. And mother is much more than breeding, but all life – and death – encompassing.

SPIRITUAL

Spirituality deals with that which is beyond the mechanical view of the physical. Here, the word "beyond" means much more than "further". It does not separate but opens to a realm that is not narrowed by a linear perception of cause and effect but bespeaks the integrated, interconnected world of source, meanings and purpose of life itself. It is thus far more expansive and at the same time more condensed and focused than what is usually associated with our apparently limited physical senses. It moves into our deeper layers of consciousness and sense of self. What causes the world to be? What underlies all that we see and experience? What is the source? And where do I fit into that larger scheme of things?

When these questions are raised, especially the last one, spirituality arises. But when these questions are answered, religion is postulated. This determines how people are dealing with the fundamental Great Fear, the existential fear of the unknown. Our beliefs about these questions form the structure of our society. How we solve problems and challenges, both individually and collectively as a society, as a culture, as political entity, and the world.

In this way, what we consider spirituality is our experiencing everything and everyone around us as inhabited with life, sentient, and requiring a relationship of love and respect, a partnership without otherization.

AUTHORITY

In reality, there is no unnatural authority. Without originating, without creating, i.e. without authorship, there is no authority, but mere dominance and control.

In reality, authority is inextricably linked to that which we have authored, that is, created. To *author* means to *create*.[9] However, the

---

[9] American Heritage Dictionary, Second College Edition, 1982.

word has been divorced from its creative root and truncated rather into dominance and impersonal 'power over', as in 'the authorities' such as judges, sheriffs, heads of government agencies and other persons who have the 'power' to take something away from us or coerce us into doing something we don't want to do.

The fundamental patriarchal re-write of life is to swap out creation for control and then pawn off control as creative rather than destructive. The term authority is thus appropriated, hollowed out and filled with the stifling, toxic air of fear.

Natural authority arises from direct connection to Source. It is self-referenced. Natural authority speaks from the inner Source and from knowing of the inner Source and from knowing of the fundamental interrelatedness between all of us. It does not dominate. Domination arises from fear engendered by a sense of powerlessness. Natural authority looks to oneself, not to others, thus has no impulse to dominate. It is self-empowered.

Woman's Natural Spiritual Authority is rooted, unadorned, and powerful because of what it is, i.e. by its very nature.

Natural authority is relational and self-referenced at the same time. It is self-arising, self-creating and responsive to the whole. It is quite simply *natural*. From her power to gestate and birth life woman continues in the natural trajectory of sustaining and nurturing that life. Natural power is interconnected with all around it. It is contextual. It is a matrix of relationships, not a vertical hierarchy of dominance and coercion.

To be self-referenced, however, does not mean self-indulgent and self-serving. To be self-referenced intrinsically includes Source, divine guidance. It does not mean not taking others into account. Quite the opposite: When we are connected to Source we include all around us because Source does.

What is natural is inherent, self-arising, self-created. It is embedded in a matrix and arises organically from power with, integral with the contents of that matrix. What is inherent, ultimately cannot be separated out, isolated and discarded. To attempt to do so damages the fabric of that matrix and what one has extracted is dead, like a hand amputated from an arm. This is what we see in artificial, unnatural authority as it operates in today's world, a dismembered "authority".

DOUBLE STANDARD OF AUTHORITY

No one questions a woman's authority and responsibility to physically nurture the child she has birthed. Then why question her authority to guide her child spiritually beyond conditioning it to conform to androcentric spiritual authority? That natural authority was usurped by men through the institution of nuclear family, marriage, and soon the male ownership and dominion over life. Marriage is an economic structure that gave man the physical and supposedly spiritual dominance over woman, her body and her children. In keeping with this development, man has tried to assert economic structure that gave men the physical and supposedly spiritual dominance over women, their bodies and their children. In keeping with this development, man has tried to assert force, control and dominion (dominance) over the Earth and attempted to state that as a divine law: "... and let them have dominion over the fish of the sea, and over the fowl of the air, and over the cattle, and over all the earth, and over every creeping thing that creeps upon the earth." (Bible, Genesis 1:26)

What would it be like to live in a world that was built on predominance values? What would it be like to live in accordance with a Natural Spiritual Authority that arises out of respect for the inherent value of each strand of the matrix of life? How would it feel to interact with an authority that is based on self-reference, self-trust, self-love, self-respect? To live by an authority which is not based in throwing someone out of the garden nor, as in the childhood game, throwing others down to make oneself "king of the hill"?

What It Is

AUTHENTIC POWER - THE FEMALE MODES OF POWER

The female mode of power, based as it is in self-authority and self-referencing, goes inward for knowledge. Being self-referenced does not mean being self-serving or self-engrossed or ignoring others. Quite the contrary, the deep self-respect it requires also demands deep respect of others. If one can source the truth from within, one knows with direct, unassailable knowing that others can do the same. This is the recognition of universal, essential divinity; it is what is meant by the Sanskrit word "namaste": "the divine within me recognizes the divine within you"; it is what is meant when Jesus said "the kingdom of god is within you" and what the Buddhists call the Buddha nature. It is therefore the kind of power and authority that does not rest on others having to be less or lower or weaker.

True authority is grounded in humility. Humus, the root word of humility, refers to the ground itself, to the soil, the source, often also called dirt, a humble word. Without dirt to hold the roots, there is no source, and we all wither and die. There can be no authority without creating, that is, no *author*ity without *author*ship, and there can be no creating that is not rooted in Source. Recognizing this is humility, for humility is simply the recognition of things as they really are, in this case the recognition of the shared, universal ground (humus) of Being.

Other than the notion of force, erroneously associated with authority, true power encompasses a much wider scope. Power is the capacity and energy to create or act. It comes and is experienced from within, while force is experienced from without.

As power is the ability to create or act, an oak tree has the power to create another oak tree. A human does not. A caterpillar has the power to become a butterfly. An oak tree does not. An apple tree has the power to create an apple while you and I cannot. We can plant an apple seed, water it, fertilize and nurture the seed to grow into a fruit bearing tree. We have all that power, but we

Authentic Power - the Female Modes of Power

cannot create an apple. Only an apple tree can do that.[10] And even the apple tree cannot do it alone. It needs earth, water, air and sunlight, the nutrients—the *matrix*—in which the apple tree can actualize her potential from the seed of herself. True power exists in a matrix of interrelationships, it is "power with"

WHY IT MATTERS

I sometimes wake up in the middle of the night with a surrealistic sense of my own good fortune. No war rages outside my bedroom window, food will be on my breakfast table, but at the same time I know that at this very moment, around the world atrocities and unspeakable suffering and brutality are being inflicted on millions of people. And millions of children are starving, thousands of them dying during the minutes I lie awake.

But before I can indulge in cynicism, I remember how Lalita Devi, Himalayan tantric mastress, reminds us that we are all ready "to explode with love". That even the most violent criminals are not exceptions, that people never reach an irreversible point.[11]

And other phrases float up in my mind from this jumble of despair and frustration:

". . shame the mothers . . into shaming their sons . . to stop raping, to stop the atrocities."

These words from Leymah Gbowee, leader of the Women of Liberia Mass Action for Peace pierce me with the iconoclastic power of Motherhood. Shame. Authentic shame, what shame really is: A

---

[10] The apple tree analogy is based on "From Sacred Blood to the Curse and Beyond" by Judy Grahn in *The Politics of Women's Spirituality: Essays on the Rise of Spiritual Power Within the Feminist Movement*, ed. Charlene Spretnak, (Anchor Press, Doubleday, Garden City, New York, 1982)

[11] Quoted in *Tantric Quest: An Encounter with Absolute Love* by Daniel Odier, (Inner Traditions Int'l., Rochester VT, 1997)

Why It Matters

call to conscience, piercing the heart, awakening feeling. The power of a mother to pierce the heart of her child. Nothing else has ever pierced my despair. But this...this could stop the insanity...this could stop the brutal rape of women...this could stop the wars: When women pierce other women's hearts and mothers pierce their sons hearts with the arrow of shame.

The words of these women speak to me with an authority that refuses to indulge the powerlessness of cynicism and despair.

All the reasons elaborated here for the importance of the Natural Spiritual Authority of Woman are mutually intertwined and inseparable, the personal, the political, the societal, and the global. The fact that life is a matrix dictates a viewpoint of the larger picture even while focussing on specifics. There can be no lasting societal significance without personal awakening. There should be no spiritual self-perception, especially not a feminist one, that considers itself insulated from society at large. (It is puzzling how much of that perception does exist, of spirituality related to the individual, to a sympathetic group or 'community' and to the 'earth' or even 'cosmos' while bypassing directly adjacent people and situations outside the comfort zone of 'community'.)

Woman's natural spiritual authority also matters because inherent in it is a common ground all peoples and nations can unify around, the values of Motherhood. Woman's natural spiritual authority offers a universal and globally unifying catalyst. Care of our children, care of our source which sustains our children: food, clean water and air. And care of what sustains the human soul: beauty, love, creativity and community.

ONLY WOMAN CAN DO IT

More than the fact that women have the power to do what life needs, there is no other source for this to happen than Woman. Therefore, women today need direct, undiluted knowledge in order to accomplish the transformation of humanity and civilization that only women can lead. Only Woman can bring humanity back into right relationship.

Why women? Because the current paradigm of authority through domination of life through force rather than a natural relationship with life is a male-identified, male-centered paradigm. The male collective consciousness has separated itself from the source of life, lost its sense of relationship, and suppressed its feeling. It is raping and pillaging the very source of life - earth and women.

Of course, this does not address individual men, many of whom are loving, and caring, nor is it a blanket statement about individual women, many of whom may act destructively and feel just as numb and disconnected as the collective male consciousness. On the deepest creature level, there is a profound difference between the doomed collective patriarchal consciousness, which is innately disconnected, and that of the individual male person, which is not. But once it started going off-course, becoming a collective, it had to formulate institutions, laws, governments, prohibitions - and religion. Like two paths that at first only diverge slightly, over time, one can no longer see "the other" path. It disappears and the path one is on seems to be the only one there is. And this is how "sole truths" come about.

And while no single woman can or would likely claim any sort of papal infallibility, Woman as the embodiment of feminine power and wisdom, endowed with the sensibilities of life-giver, indeed can and should know herself collectively as the only true authority. What is needed is the reassertion of Woman's collective consciousness, a collective wisdom that far exceeds the wisdom of any individual person. As no single male human should be made to bear the burden of patriarchal destruction, women cannot really do this working in isolation, but rather by resting in Woman as the collective, inclusive source.

Such a collective consciousness includes the morphic resonance that reverberates just beneath the surface of our experience as the

Why It Matters

hidden, but ever-living stream from the tens of thousand of years of Woman's spiritual and cultural leadership.

WHY IT MATTERS ON A PERSONAL LEVEL

For Women Themselves

To name it and to claim it: Woman's Natural Spiritual Authority. That act of claiming it liberates a woman. It breaks the contrived conceptual chains of dis-empowerment, the acquired habits of self denigrating thoughts and feelings, the demonization of our female body. It helps us remedy the debilitating effects of dismemberment, of alienation from our own body, from the rejuvenating power of our menses, from self love, from the community of women. It helps to stop the draining of our psychic energy and creativity which results from this dismemberment.

It helps us realize our marginalization as Woman from the crucial issues of the age and the devastating impact this is having on humanity. We wake up! Stepping into in our natural spiritual authority we move ourselves from the margin to the center of the world stage. Here, we stand in solidarity with Woman's collective power and wisdom of the ages. Here, we restore the world to sanity.

If we feel the conditioned self-doubt and self-loathing stir inside us, we can direct our attention away from such external reference and re-align with the intrinsic truth of our womanly nature. We unshackle ourselves from the false authority that would coerce us into negation of our nature and birthright, we reference our self, we *woman-identify*. We come back into conscious relationship with all that is. 'All that is' represents no trendy new-age term but the scientifically corroborated reality. Based in this reality, we orient ourselves within the unbroken lineage of Woman as embodiment of the Great Mother Creator. We call ourselves back to the natural relationship of woman to man, Woman gives man life. Woman is the Creator of humanity both female and male.

Why it Matters on a Societal Level

Natural spiritual authority of woman also translates into the individual personal lives of women. In the modern family structure, built upon patriarchal tenets, the man is the "head" of the family and the woman is to obey him. It is impossible to know how much benefit to humanity has been lost because women have labored in the confines of the enforced nuclear family, separated from women, from the female collective. Women's time and creative energy are drained into the inordinate burdens of raising children in isolation without the support of the proverbial village it takes to raise a child. A further loss is caused due to women's internalization of other ubiquitous misogynous "spiritual" teachings. The loss is truly incalculable.

It has not always been this way and it is certainly not natural. It is yet another patriarchal reversal. Ammachi, the 'hugging saint of India' has pointed out:

"In ancient India, the terms that were used by a husband when talking about his wife were, 'the one who leads the husband through life' and 'the one who guides her husband on the path of righteousness'."

A woman is the natural spiritual authority of not only her children, but also her mate or husband. Shocking as this may be to women oriented to the male-identified religions, it is a simple fact of history.

WHY IT MATTERS ON A SOCIETAL LEVEL

One of the dimensions of the natural spiritual authority of woman that sometimes veers from sight is the generational significance, how it affects Her children, the next generation of those who shape the next generation, the role models, be it as parents, workers, teachers, politicians, artists, scientists and spiritual leaders.

Society gives credence, a kind of credibility 'credit', to those most closely resembling the popular image of the divine. With only

Why It Matters

a male image of the divine, and the female, at best, relegated to it's 'immaculate', de-sexed mother 'aspect', only a male can assert spiritual authority. For this to change and for the Goddess/Women's/Feminist Spirituality movement to progress in its vision, women must restore a female image of the divine.

The Goddess and/or woman honoring roots of all religion are more than amply evident in virtually all anthropological and archeological research, unless the researchers insist on interpreting a tree as a weapon – as in the frequent misinterpretation of a tree as an arrow. The fact is that in the Paleolithic era for every one sculpture of a male there were 100 of females.

But that Woman honoring root has been obscured by the Great Reversal, through creation myths wherein males imitate motherhood and where the female is described as coming from the male, spiritual tales which justify male authority to the exclusion of female authority. This sanctions male domination.

By recognizing that woman's spiritual authority is natural, a woman can re-open the channel of understanding her power as arising from the very root of her being. What is natural cannot really be taken away, only obscured. She may remember a gut-level feeling of knowing that her power required no reference to external validation or definition. She may remember her power as being beyond modern societal norms and distortions, beyond her personal conditioning. She places herself in an evolutionary context that predates the contrivance of male spiritual authority, a context of centuries of the natural functioning of woman's spiritual authority and woman's authorship of spirituality, culture, art and science. She recognizes herself as the originator of human society.

Once a woman recognizes this, she unveils for herself a vision for guiding society back to the values of that original society. She can pass these original societal values on to the next generation, her daughters and sons. This was a society in which Woman's natural spiritual authority manifested a "natural religion" born of love, protection, nurturance and guidance not only for her physical children, the life she has created, but for all life.

Woman created the cultural mores, the expressions of spiritual feeling and communion through dance, song, ritual, through beauty and art in ceramics, textiles, clothing. She is the originator of the shamanic healing arts, the original medicine.

Much of this grew out of not only Woman's nurturing of life, her children, but out of her contact with the invisible worlds of spirit, her visioning, dreaming and collective visioning through the sisterhood of her sacred bloods. A cadre of tribal women bleeding in harmony with the moon cycle and each other amplified each woman's capacity to bring forth the wisdom of the womb, to amplify this incomparable portal to Spirit and to other dimensions, and from Spirit into incarnation. The blood mysteries of Woman, as we will see, led to the origins of science, measurement discovered through Woman's awe-inspiring alignment with the cyclic moon.

The natural extension of values based on Woman's natural spiritual authority is love, inclusiveness, and freedom. Reclaimed by Woman and seen in this light, spirituality, culture, art and science may serve as a vehicle away from the materialistic alienation and toward right relationship.

WHY IT MATTERS ON A GLOBAL LEVEL

Spiritual values are what determines structure and content of our culture, our art, laws, education, institutions, family structure. They determine how we treat Earth and each other. The rationales for violence, sex trade, the inhumane, brutal treatment of animals in research and in factory farming rest ultimately in spiritual dogmas of separation. This is the only way to sustain them. And this is why the spiritual must consider itself political.

Why It Matters

Mass Action for Peace: Leymah Gbowee

In Liberia, only a few years ago, when people were being massacred by the tens of thousands, when rape was commonplace and children were starving, when a woman and her mother survived nights hiding huddled in the dark hearing the screams of hundreds of people being slaughtered outside their home, that woman, Leymah Gbowee had a "silly dream" (her term) in which she was told to gather women in chanting, dance and prayer, to end that civil war.

She shared her dream with others but felt unworthy to be the one to organize and lead it. "Not me!" she said but the other women said she was the one to lead. Gbowee was the "author" of the dream. The power resided in her.

For three years Gbowee and the Women of Liberia demanded peace negotiations.[12] Their headquarters, an open air fish market, their uniforms bright white T-shirts meant to catch the eye of the officials and media driving by. Their "weapons" were song, dance, prayer, protest signs and the collective power of women working in solidarity, often standing arm in arm, a weave of female power. Gbowee herself says their "greatest weapons" were "moral clarity, persistence, and patience". For three years they unceasingly protested. "Wherever they were, we were there," Gbowee said. "We were all over them!" She described it as "peaceful, feminine havoc".

When peace negotiations finally began, Gbowee and a long line of women traveled to Ghana and stood there, arm in arm, in the hall outside the negotiations room. When the peace talks broke down they *demanded* that the talks continue until there was resolution, whereupon the police threatened to arrest Gbowee for "obstructing justice". That was, she says, like gas on an open flame. "I just went wild...'Ok, I'm going to make it very, very easy for you to

---

[12] *Pray the Devil Back to Hell*, documentary film produced by Abigail Disney, directed by Gini Reticker, Fork Films, LLC, 2008.

Why It Matters on a Global Level

arrest me.' "I took off my hair tie...'I'm going to strip naked.[13] Gbowee made use of an ancient cultural power of African women: To strip naked in public is a feared curse resulting in absolute bad fortune. The rest of the women left no doubt they were ready to do the same.

The men returned to the conference room and continued the negotiations. Two weeks later, the terms of the peace treaty were announced. The warlord president of Liberia, Charles Taylor, was exiled.

Gbowee's "silly dream" generated not only a successful mass action for peace, but generated another, unprecedented phenomenon, Christian and Muslim women set aside mutual distrust, crossed the religious divide and acted in spiritual unity. They did it for the sake of the children, Gbowee says[14]. Motherhood knows no borders, it transcends nations, races and religions.

The Spiritual Mandates the Political

The collective power of Woman does not need guns, military structure, coercion by threat of death or imprisonment. Woman as a collective has power, true power. True power grows from what is small, the oak from the acorn, the human body from the egg, the river from the spring, the ocean from the river, a raging fire from a spark. Mass action for peace from a "silly dream".

And though Gbowee said that they deliberately kept it from being political and only spoke out "for peace" without political criticisms of the president, warlord Charles Taylor, at the root of the whole movement is the reality that the spiritual *is* political. In fact, more political, than politics. The results, successful peace negotiations, the exile of Taylor from Liberia and the installation of a

---

[13] http://www.pbs.org/moyers/journal/06192009/transcript1.html

[14] http://www.thedailybeast.com/blogs-and-stories/2010-07-07/with-leymah-gbowee-building-a-congolese-womens-movement/

woman president testify to this. It shows that the natural spiritual authority of Woman is stronger than ordinary politics. Dreaming, praying, dancing, singing and chanting, and doing this in solidarity, collectively as women, these are the methods of shamans, priestesses, healers and female spiritual leaders.

Innate spiritual authority trumps decreed political authority. Spiritual authority encompasses political authority, determines the nature of political authority for political authority is an extension of spiritual values. The Liberian women's Mass Action for Peace stepped "outside the political box". The women's actions were based in spiritual values and sustained by spiritual practices. Had they only worked from political means, protest alone, or as is done in most movements for justice, through the laws, they may not have been successful. I believe the emotional and spiritual nourishment of dancing, singing and praying was crucial in keeping their vision and determination alive, moving them past the inevitable moments of disappointment and fatigue and giving them the fuel to sustain "the demand".

Gbowee admonishes women to make what she calls *the demand*. That without it women "are failing slowly":

"We need to start demanding in the most radical sense, our respect, the respect of our daughters, sisters and best friends. We also need to include a demand for our space, our time and bring to an end every other thing that has contributed to violating us through policies, practices and traditions."[15]

This is unapologetic spiritual authority.

Gbowee is also employing two other female powers. The first is the power of the female body over the male psyche. Towards the end of the three year protest the Christian and Muslim women joined together in a sex strike. They told their men that even

---

[15] http://peaceisloud.org/wp/peace-builders-leymah-gbowee

though they were not actively engaged in the war, if they were not *actively engaged to end it*, they would get no sex.

Woman's holistic sensibility between the physical and spiritual, the authorship of life and the responsibility to protect it could never be more clear. In essence they were saying, *if you don't actively fight, as I am, to protect life, you have no access to the source of that life, my body!"* Needless to say, many men started contributing to the Mass Action for Peace.

Finally, as she turns her focus to ending the mass rape in the Democratic Republic of Congo, Gbowee is calling for women to assert yet another female power: "We must shame the mothers of the marauders into shaming their sons, into demanding an end to the marauding, an end to the rape, and an end to the atrocities."[16] This is shame for what it authentically is, an arrow to wake up Mother Mind. to pierce the heart, to feel.

MYTH—THE STORY WE TELL IS THE WORLD WE MAKE

The collective consciousness and behavior, the customs, the laws and institutions of a society, all are determined by the story it tells about itself and the world, its creation myth, its spiritual cosmology, its answers to the questions "where do we come from?" and "why are we here?" and "where are we going?" and "What is our relationship to the cosmos, the earth and each other?"

In the modern world, a number of variations of one story dominate the globe, the myth that a male god created us and therefore man — rather than woman — is authorized by god to run the world. This myth eventually plays out, as we see it now, after a few thousand years, on the downward arc of its trajectory, in pervasive actions of misogyny, of violence against women, starvation of children and the pollution of our source of life, Earth.

---

[16] Ibid. www.thedailybeast.com

Myth—the Story We Tell is the World We Make

Unfortunately, a majority of people has chosen to believe that war, violence and male domination are the way it has always been. Most people equate the terms "ancient" and "traditional" with that story, which leaves no avenues out of today's destructive paradigm. To believe propaganda will increasingly dissociate us from reality and bar us from realistic solutions.

SHAKTI MYTH

A very good example of the battle between the old and the new myths is found in the Devi Bhagavata Purana, a primary text in the Hindu tradition of the Divine Mother. In an episode, the great gods Shiva and Vishnu are attacked by a mighty army of demons, and, in an extended battle, it takes the joint forces of both, Shiva and Vishnu, to vanquish them. But despite that victory being the result of joint forces, they are both so vain as to claim it to be their individual victory and boast about their prowess before their respective Shaktis, the two goddesses, Parvati and Lakshmi.

The two Shaktis find the situation quite ludicrous and laugh at Shiva's and Vishnu's naiveté. Their inflated egos thus punctured, the gods become angry and address their spouses rudely. As a result, the goddesses immediately vanish and, as this happens, the world plunges into turmoil.

Without the power of their Shaktis, the two gods became powerless and fall into a lifeless, confused state. Only after an extended period of severe penance does the Great Goddess (Shakti) restore herself to the two gods, saying:

> "The insult shown towards my manifestations has led to this calamitous state. Such a crime should never again be committed."
>
> (Devi Bhagavata Purana: 7.29.25)

Shiva and Vishnu, now devoid of inflated pride, return to their previous natures and are thus able to perform their godly functions as before.

"If abandoned by me, this universe becomes motionless. If I leave Shiva, he will not be able to kill demons. A weak man is declared to be without any Shakti, nobody says that he is without Shiva, or without Vishnu. Those who are timid, afraid, or under one's enemies they are all called Shakti-less; no one says that this man is Shiva less and so forth."

"So, the creation that you are about to perform, know Shakti to be the cause thereof. When you will be endowed with that Shakti, you will be able to create the world. Vishnu, Shiva, Indra, Agni, Moon, Sun, Death, and all the other deities are able to do their karmas only when they are united with their respective Shaktis. This earth, when united with Shakti, remains fixed and becomes capable to hold all beings inhabiting it. If it be devoid of this power, it cannot support even an atom."

(Devi Bhagavata Purana: 3.6)

Such a male god, boasting about his powers as if he existed apart from his own birth by the Goddess is a frequent theme in myths, and it is not exclusive to India. We find it, for instance, in the tale of Gilgamesh referenced further below, and the Australian aboriginal men confess to their "stealing woman's power when the women were not looking.

MYTHS OF MALE MOTHERHOOD

There are quite a number of myths which explicitly or by inference claim a male origin of life. The story told in Genesis is the creation myth that justifies male domination in most western societies.

Adam and Eve

The name Eve means "Mother of All Living". The Old Testament, however, gives us the myth of the Garden of Eden where a male god gives birth to woman (Eve) by way of a man's (Adam's) rib. This doctrine of male 'birth' is the basis for thousands of years of male "spiritual authority" which has provided the justification for just as many years of male political, economic, and social dominance. This

Myth—the Story We Tell is the World We Make

version of 'manifest destiny' is fashioned from the reversal of reality, a reversal, which invades every phase of life, every social institution, the global economy, and every nation and government today. Male domination and its effects are global in scope. Its roots lie in a conceptualized, disconnected and imposed male spiritual authority that is severed from Source. Instead of reverence for woman as life giver, a male god declares himself the source of life, the source of the female, and brands that female as bringer of death and sin into the world, the spoiler of his once perfect garden.

Eve and Adam

Language offers a simple explanation why Woman and Serpent had to be painted as evil by the same brush: The words for Serpent, Eve and Teacher are cognates of each other in the Aramaic language. In "*Lady and the Beasts*", Buffie Johnson refers to early Christian Gnostic texts with many hidden references to the serpent's superior wisdom. Appearing in the form of word play that equates the serpent with the instructor (*serpent* = hewa; *to instruct* = hawa). Other Gnostic accounts add a four-way pun that includes how Eve (Hawwah) instead of tempting Adam gives life to him and instructs him.[17]

This, of course, was not a consequence of linguistic coincidence. Rather the linguistic facts were a consequence of the reality. Johnson points out that the story in Genesis is a projection and cover-up for Yahweh's transgression against his creator Hawwah (Eve), her sacred serpent and his stealing her power and even her name, as his own name suggests.[18]

---

[17] Buffie Johnson, *Lady of the Beasts: Ancient Images of the Goddess and Her Sacred Animals*, (HarperCollins, New York, NY, 1988), page 191

[18] Ibid.

Myths of Male Motherhood

When Woman is demoted from leading with the civilizing, humanizing, refining aspect of her being, "civilization" takes on the brutal, pain inflicting qualities it now has. Without feeling, without a connection, the sense of wonder at life numbs down to a dead sensorium, trust and joy suffocate under fear driven control, reverence bloats to arrogance, and self-honesty or self-reflection are crushed under the boot of self-deceit.

Without the refinement of woman's sexual-sensual body knowledge, societies are left with the trajectory of the truncated, male capacity when it is split off from these sensitivities and their resonance in relationships, not only between women and men but between adults and children and all of life. Women have been separated from their bodies by the demonization of our natural capacity for nuanced, powerful and emotionally-sensually-spiritually integrated sexual pleasure, through body loathing for not being able to measure up to the emaciated, under-nourished, pre-pubescent looking bodies of "top models", by fear of fat, by fashion and by a large spectrum of personal and institutionalized physical and emotional abuse. The results at the end of such a trajectory range from the "soft" abuse as propagated in modern fashion, in cosmetics - including the newly fashionable practices of genital and anal "bleaching" - and the advertising media in general, to the ubiquitous domestic violence, child abuse, the escalating brutality through rape, sexual abuse, and the separation from ourselves by pornographic violence of video games and the real, all to real "game" of war as portrayed in extensive high production value advertisement for military institutions.

All this aims at eradicating feeling. War and rape packaged as video games brutalize generations. One cannot rape what one feels.

THE GODDESS ROOTS OF ALL RELIGION

For hundreds of thousands of years, the power of the womb and body was revered universally by humankind as the Great Mother, the Goddess. Feminine Power embodied in Woman is undoubtedly the foundation of all religion. Before there was ever a concept of a male god, an idea that arose only 9,000 years ago, there was the Great Goddess. Before Allah was Al-Lat. Before Yahweh was Asherah (and Hawwah). Before Mary and Jesus was Isis and Horus of Egypt. Before Buddha was the Mother of the Buddhas.

A quick nutshell of religious history is that first there was the Goddess. Then Her consort son was acknowledged. The consort son was promoted to sitting next to Her on a dual throne. Then he became King beside Her and she was his Queen. She also became the throne upon which he sat. Before the king could rule, he needed to have the authorization of the Goddess/Priestess. Later, patriarchy did away with Her authority altogether, claiming the "divine right of kings", an authority supposedly derived from a male god with no Goddess in sight.

One particular example of that history as found in many cultures is the image of the lioness - which, as we know, is an epiphany of the Goddess and also closely associated with the throne. If we follow that image through time and trace how it changed, what we see is the usurpation of woman's power. Goddess iconography is replete with lionesses: The Sumerian Goddess Lilith stands on the back of lionesses; Hindu Goddess Durga rides a lioness; the traditional Sanskrit word for throne is *singhasana*, 'seat of a lion'; lionesses flank the throne of Cybele of Anatolia (ancient Turkey) and the Cretan Goddess standing high on a hill; lions adorn the walls and entrance arches of the Babylonian Temple of Ishtar; an image of Medusa giving birth shows her flanked by lionesses; Sekhmet, the Egyptian Goddess of the Sun, Childbirth and Healing is usually depicted as a woman with a lioness head. Even into the era of the

Catholic Mary, an occasional painting will depict her seated on a lion throne.

Eventually the lionesses become the male "lion king", from Richard the Lion-Hearted to the modern-day Disney cartoon character. The king sits upon Her former seat of power. The Bible describes King Solomon's throne as flanked by two lions at the armrests and twelve more on either side; male lions emblazon the crests of royalty; statues of male lions today sit at entrances of wealthy estates or mansions.

The reason for looking closely at the myths and mechanisms of patriarchal force and domination is not to inflate the already immense grudge humanity could have against patriarchy into a billowing sail that would take us nowhere fast. The real benefit lies in recognizing the nearly seamless fabric of fundamental reversals covering our perception of reality. Beneath that cover, nearly all what makes the "Original Religion" is fully intact. In fact, we are looking at patriarchal characteristics with new glasses to discover what was stolen from women.

PARTHENOGENESIS — PRE-PATRIARCHAL GENESIS

At its origin then it follows that the most ancient myths of the Goddess refer to Her power of parthenogenesis, that She is self-created; She gives birth to Herself. In the legacy of the Great Mother, all power ultimately resides in Her. As a noun, the word 'author' is also defined as "God"[19]. In light of parthenogenesis, this definition takes on a reclaimed historical meaning. and reflects the essence of self-referencing, of Woman's natural spiritual authority.

Considering such a scope of authorship, the misogynist agenda in even contemplating anything like an "illegitimate birth" can only be plausible if the creation of life is appropriated by a man-made legal system, that of requiring women to be separated and each

---

[19] American Heritage Dictionary, Second College Edition

The Goddess Roots of All Religion

become subject to a male. How can any birth be illegitimate? Any child born of woman is legitimate, a child of the Mother, a holy child. Only in a death culture such as one that blames Eve for 'man' falling out of the garden into death, could it be interpreted otherwise.

Parthenogenetic authorship of life is also expressed in the pre-Vedic cosmology of India. In her book *Sakhiyani* Giti Thadani describes this mythic personification of the universe as Twin Sisters, the *Jami* sisters. They are apparently "opposite" to each other, one is day, the other night, one is light, the other dark, one moist, one dry, one is stillness, the other is motion. Yet, these opposites are not in dualistic, static opposition, rather they meet and transform fluidly into each other through a triadic *third* aspect. This third aspect through which the one sister becomes the other, is the womb space. The naturally occurring polarities of positive-negative, or yin and yang, are not divided into masculine and feminine, but are dynamic, fluid aspects of the great cyclic round of the Feminine. The Feminine is the wholeness which encompasses, gives birth to and transforms the polarities within herself. For millennia this womb space has been and continues to be represented in Hindu mandalas and yantras by the downward pointing triangle, the geometric representation of woman's womb and pudendum.

This sheds a whole new light on the subject of trinity and how many re-writes of the original wholeness of the Feminine occur in other traditions around the world. The completeness of the Goddess is dismembered into male and female or even all male; female deities become anemic "aspects of" or are changed to male; or the once pre-eminent female deity is demoted to a mere "consort of" a male god.[20]

---

[20] Paula Gunn Allen names a number of reversals of female to male creator gender changes in the Native American cosmologies in her book *The Sacred Hoop: Recovering the Feminine in American Indian Traditions*, (Beacon Press, Boston, MA, 1986), p. 41

DISMEMBERMENT OF THE GODDESS

To sustain the level of insanity evident in the civilization today—the fact that we are on course to destroy our own source (Mother)—the underlying myth must be one of separation.

The myth goes something like this: The physical and spiritual, the natural and divine, are separate from each other. The physical (body and nature) is polluted with evil. God wants us to be spiritual and in order to be spiritual we must overcome the physical. Nature can and should be overcome and controlled.

God gave us dominion over the earth. We are supposed to be separate from and superior to all of nature.

Woman has frequently been described in patriarchal religious dogma as the passive field where the man plants his life-giving seed. Thus, man's three second contribution is elevated to the level of "life source" while the woman's nine months of gestation, not to mention her hours of life-risking labor, years of breast feeding, and general Motherhood of the entire family are relegated to the inconsequential and passive. Could there be any more absurd reversal?

Such a reversal is only possible because this field/seed analogy is based in fiction. It epitomizes how far from reality the seed dogma is which demotes Earth as inconsequential and passive, as if "the field" had no life of its own, had nothing to contribute to the seed except to be a location, as if the soil were not teeming with the vital nutrients and the protective darkness essential to the seed becoming anything more than an agglomeration of dry carbohydrates.

In reality, the seed receives its very existence from the Earth, just as man receives his existence from Woman. Who births man in the first place that he exists to have "seed"? And thus we come full circle from dogma back to reality.

The Goddess Roots of All Religion

The myth that leads to dismemberment of the Mother Creator plays out like this: Male attraction to the female body gets demonized and projected onto women who must be controlled. The physical which is "polluted with evil" becomes a self-fulfilling prophecy: We pollute the air, water and earth. Men pollute women with demonization, rape and oppression. Nature is dominated, forced to grow in unnatural extreme conditions which in agriculture require poisons and artificial fertilizers and in animal factory farms require hormones to force growth and antibiotics to quell diseases fostered by animals packed into cages too small for them to move.

Dams are built to control rivers and produce electricity regardless of ecosystems, clouds are seeded to produce rain when and where we want it. Seeds and species are patented, nature is under corporate ownership. DNA, life, is genetically modified to conform to our agenda which views itself superior to billions of years of evolution. Women's wombs are governed by law, better yet, replaced by test tubes.

While a thorough list would seem endless and is very familiar to many, it is not redundant to repeat some of it here, because it is how the dismemberment of the Goddess plays out in our daily lives.

Among the mythological equivalents, perhaps the most easily recognizable example of this is the Greek version of Aphrodite. Originally the Anatolian (ancient Turkey) Great Mother of Life and Death, She was eventually reduced to a petty, jealous beauty-queen "goddess of love".

A lesser known but more telling example is told in the Sumerian tale of Gilgamesh, where the male hero-god Marduk cuts his mother Tiamat's body in two and from it "creates" heaven and earth (two *separate* realms). This act ignores the fact that She, his mother, had already created the (*whole*) world, including heaven and earth, and including Marduk himself. Patriarchal religion cre-

The Goddess of Laussel

ates a second creation, based in the dismembering of Woman and Goddess and the erection of a male god in their place.

The notion of equating matricide with the origin of the world is perpetuated in modern psychology, for example by the Swiss psychiatrist Carl Jung's view that in order for a man to mature he must commit psychic matricide.

THE GODDESS OF LAUSSEL

Only a mile from the famous Caves of Lascaux in southern France, the so-called 'Goddess of Laussel' was found. Some historians and androcentric scholars wish to relegate the about 22,000

The Goddess Roots of All Religion

year old art to a fractured 'Venus' of Laussel or even a mere 'fertility symbol'. And even thus reduced, she is not found in the history books in school. Perhaps this is because, in reality, she is an icon of Woman's natural spiritual authority.

She holds one of the earliest calendars of humanity, a bison horn notched with thirteen lines for the thirteen moon cycles of the year. It is lifted in her right hand while her left hand rests on her corpulent belly, pointing to her womb. This is the source of her knowledge.

It is also the source of the calendar she holds, the measurement of time, the beginning of math and science. Women's observation of the synchronicity of their menses with the Moon was the basis for math, science, and astronomy. Language reflects this in the words menses, moon, month, measure, meter, all cognates of each other. Measurement of time, distance and quantity dawned on human consciousness through Woman's cyclic womb connection to the waxing and waning moon. The word "mathematics" literally means "wisdom (themis) of the mothers (ma)". It was not a dry abstraction, a disembodied concept, but a vital, reality-bound awareness that rose up out of the blood rich body of the mothers.

Thus, this full figured guardian of the sacred cavern, the temple, stood in authoritative position at the entrance of the sacred cavern

The Goddess of Laussel

temple. To enter the cave, one had to pass by her and her reminder of Woman as the originator of a distinctly human relationship to the cosmos through Woman's womb.

Her presence as guardian of the cave declares:

> *here you enter the sacred temple of Woman's spiritual physical link to the Moon, Time and the Cosmos. You enter the cave womb of the Great Mother of whom Woman is the embodiment.*

"Essentialism"

In answering some scholars who would classify this image as a mere biological schematic, and who criticize the Goddess movement as "essentialist", I would like to refer to Max Dashu's article "The Meanings of Goddess".[21] After all, if the symbolism of womb and moon cycle as represented in the Goddess of Laussel were merely about biological reality it would not be carved at the entrance of a cave. Caves were the original temples. What it really is, is a depiction of the essence of woman's sacred body.

This pre-historic and historic reverence of woman's body as being sacred often clashes abruptly with the modern theory of "essentialism". Max Dashu, independent scholar and creatrix of the 'Suppressed Histories Archives', who has built a collection of some 15,000 slides and 100 shows depicting women's social, spiritual and cultural power and leadership, points out that

> *For at least twenty years the Goddess movement has been assailed as "essentialist" by post-modernist theorists. They mean that an innate female essence is being claimed, in a biological determinism and rigid gender categorization.*

---

[21] http://www.goddesspages.co.uk/index.php?option=com_content&task =view&id=459 See also Max Dashu's website: Suppressed Histories Archives: Real women, global vision http://www.suppressedhistories.net

The Goddess Roots of All Religion

"Innate female essence", according to Dashu, is mistaken for *"biological determinism and rigid gender categorization"*.

And there is another reason, Max Dashu says, why women recoil from the idea of "essentialism", the fear that, *"gendered symbolism locks women into the very categories that lie at the root of their oppression."*

The white elephant here is a deeply internalized reversal. Indeed, one could see the nature of the oppression as based in the males' lack of femaleness rather than the femaleness bearing any resemblance to a deficiency.

Max Dashu says that not only have they *lost sight of the Mystery, the real "essence"* but there is a terror cultivated of anything that fails to fit in boxes or words. And she continues: *"We reaffirm embodiment as sacred, in the face of a long history of deprecating the body-especially the female body, whose sacred symbolism has been expropriated, colonized in myriad ways, and reconfigured as "obscene." To confuse this transformative reclamation with "essentialism" misunderstands and distorts its meaning.*

Dashu speaks of *the soulful nature of things, including matter itself,* and continues: *This goes to the realm of Mystery: real experiences and insights that can't be explained in words, only perceived by our right brain consciousness. We don't reject the rational, but wholeness demands that we learn to reintegrate it with the totality of our awareness, including its mythic and melodic aspects, the dream consciousness.*

These concepts *"grow from the spiritual ground that predates the consolidation of the "major religions" that people are fighting over now, a division that separated the religious and secular, everyday life, sexuality and death, from the sacred.*

The Goddess of Laussel embodies the essence of woman's sacred body and her natural spiritual authority.

The Hunt as Spiritual Act - Prey is not Other

Another compelling illustration of the comprehensive mutuality of the relationship between womb and the rest of reality is seen in the Mesolithic picture below, engraved on rock walls in the Algerian Sahara (around 12,000 BCE).

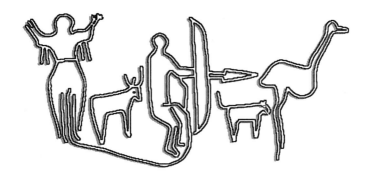

In her book, *Lady of the Beasts*,[22] the ground-breaking author Buffie Johnson describes this view of the Goddess of the Hunt as the hunter being entirely dependent for a successful kill upon the line of power flowing from the womb of the woman to and through his sex, arms and weapon.

Once we know the cycle of life, death and rebirth we can recognize that the life sustaining death of the animal is linked to the cyclic life, death and rebirth dynamic of the womb.

The hunt depicted here is not an isolated act of killing, nor is it an exclusively male undertaking. Hunting was a spiritual act. By implication of the woman's uplifted hands, this drawing acknowledges the involvement of the woman/priestess, connected and connecting to the greater powers of which she is the embodiment.

---

[22] Buffie Johnson, Lady of the Beasts: Ancient Images of the Goddess and Her Sacred Animals, (HarperCollins, New York, NY, 1988), page 19

Hunting, eating, mating, birthing and burying, all was sacred in the cycle of life. Death was not the evil disruption of God's perfect plan. Rather, the strands of our individual lives were felt and known as inseparable from the web of what sustained our lives.

And, in the midst of all this life and death and rebirth is Woman, the matrix who bled from a wound that did not cause death but rather was the blood of life.

SHAMANS, PRIESTESSES, HEALERS, MIDWIVES, MEDICINE WOMEN

Woman's relational power does not arise only from her capacity to birth children. Her innate connection to life extends beyond biological motherhood. That is the source of the patriarchal terror of woman. The biological mother hood is part and source of the matrix of a larger scope of motherhood, the motherhood of humanity's spirituality, culture and art, all which arose out of woman's blood knowledge. Woman's monthly bleeding puts her in touch with cosmic cycles, the celestial round of stars, moons and planets.

"Woman is by nature a shaman" is a proverb of the Chukchee, a tribe located in northeastern Siberia where the word "shaman" originates. Shamans heal, guide, protect, bring wisdom. Titles and functions akin to shaman are curanderos, medicine women, healers, witches, midwives, priestesses.

The fact that woman gives birth tends to make her an excellent leader of her people. The one who gives life is most likely revere and nurture it and conversely less likely to destroy it. War has never been a woman's game. Woman knows the cyclic reality of life and death every month with her menses, she knows the price of gestation, of growing a whole, separate body inside her own, she knows the pain and joy of child birth, the intimacy of feeding from her own body. Like pregnancy, for Woman the sexual act itself is one of opening and encompassing, expanding herself to include another.

Shamans, Priestesses, Healers, Midwives, Medicine Women

Women's spirituality is rooted in the body. Women's religion, the original human religion, has always been ecstatic in the sense of being "beyond the little personality". It encompassed spirit and flesh as a double spiral, inseparably entwined within each other, a double

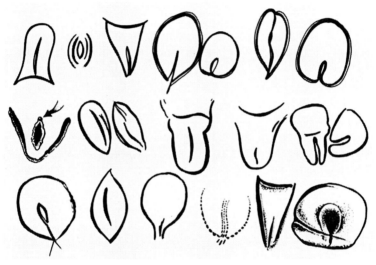

Paleolithic Vulva Images

helix of creation and pleasure. It was a natural religion that interacted with sun, moon and seasons, with the ascent and descent of light and dark; with planting, harvesting and replanting, with life, death and rebirth. The observation of the natural cycles gave rise to agriculture, rituals, dance, science, and song.

This essential connection to the natural world was reflected and expressed in the historic and pre-historic devotional depictions of woman's vulva and body, animals, plants and the patterns of natural energy expressed on pottery and textiles in the form of spirals, circles, triangles, chevrons, double and tri lines, and curvilinear designs.

Three Spiritual Dynamics of Woman's Body

The Womb as Physical Creator

The womb as source and author of humanity in a physical way is self-evident. But it encompasses much more than in other mammals.

Because of the spherical and holistic nature of Woman's sensual awareness she experiences sexuality and spirituality as a continuum of deep feeling, caring and ecstasy. For Woman, sexual pleasure is not limited to procreation but is linked to both heart and life. She bonds with her lover, she bonds with her offspring. It is natural for a woman to feel deeply when she is making love, when she is bleeding in her menses, when she is holding or breast-feeding her baby. Women have even reported feeling orgasmic while giving birth. These feelings go beyond procreation and are spiritual experiences arising from her spherical sensate awareness.

There is a physiological context for these feelings. Whether cuddling her baby or her mate, Woman's body is flooded with oxytocin, a hormone that activates emotional bonding. This hormone lingers in a woman's body for a much longer time than in the male body, which quickly diminishes oxytocin with testosterone. A woman's social experience remains expanded and enriched much longer than that of a statistically average male.

The Womb as Author and Channel of Spiritual Life

The womb is an organ not only of physical creativity but of psychic perception as well. It - or should we say 'She'? - physically creates flesh from spirit, *and* she psychically brings wisdom and guidance into this world, for the people, from spirit. Thus, the womb is a portal not only for birthing bodies but also for manifesting spiritual knowledge, a spherical source of inner vision, making Woman the natural shaman.

The Womb as Author and Channel of Spiritual Life

The physiological process that preeminently participates in making the womb a channel of spiritual knowledge and insight is a woman's monthly bleeding. When she is in menses, a woman's outer senses are slightly dulled; the body calls out for more rest, stillness and quiet to accommodate the heightened inner, psychic perception. It is a natural state of meditation. Without this quiet, women may experience the so-called pre-menstrual syndrome. PMS is often related to the body's response to ignoring and countering the natural introversion of the cycle.

The ovum is dying and the womb is shedding the blood-enriched tissue that would have nourished it. This is a regular descent, a shamanic opening, an involution down and in, to an inner connection to reality. The 'eye of the womb', the pineal gland, also seen as third eye so often depicted on Indian Goddesses, is now active, looking into the inner worlds, dreaming. With that pineal gland connection, the womb becomes the conduit of the dreamtime, of visioning and the gathering of wisdom.

Just as the stars are only visible at night in the darkness, so can women see further into the interior and immensely larger dimension of reality in this dark time of death and transition. As the veil between dimensions thins, the communication between the them increases. This communication with the unseen dimensions - or worlds - is the province of the shaman.

It is this power that prompted tribal women to jointly remove themselves from regular daily activities to a moon lodge (menstrual hut) during their menses to dream and to receive visioning through the sisterhood of their sacred bloods, to receive guidance for themselves and for their people. For this reason, some cultures see

The Female Body in Totality as 'Calibrator of Reality'.

Three spiritual dynamics of woman's body

FEMALE SPIRITUAL TANTRIC TEACHERS

An explicit example of this view of Woman as superior guide and her Natural Spiritual Authority is found in medieval (eighth through twelfth centuries) Tantric Buddhism where Female spiritual tantric teachers were considered 'qualified' on the basis of their natural authority, the reality of the power and knowledge they held and gathered disciples based on their actual accomplishments rather than an outside credential. Women in the Tantric scriptures were regarded with great homage and respect the initiatresses of enlightenment. Tantric Buddhist practitioner, scholar and author Miranda Shaw documents in her book *Passionate Enlightenment: Women in Tantric Buddhism* that women were the actual founders of Tantric Buddhism as all the male "founders" had female teachers. She further points out that women held spiritual authority based on their actual accomplishments in meditation and subtle yogas and without the need or desire for formal ordination. These women, as their biographies reveal, did not hesitate to unapologetically puncture men's bloated self-image or reprimand them in their prejudices or self deceit.[23]

Over time, however, since female sexuality is by nature integral to spiritual awareness and a woman's self-reliant authority, demonizing it was the only way for male religion to dominate. This is the fundamental dismemberment perpetrated by male-identified religion.

The superiority of encompassing authority compared to decreed power is "wired" into Woman and women's relational approach to power. Recent research shows that when women listen to someone speaking, both hemispheres of her brain are active whereas in men only the left hemisphere is active. Women perceive holistically, undivided. Feeling and thinking, the right brain and the

---

[23] Miranda Shaw, *Passionate Enlightenment: Women in Tantric Buddhism*, (Princeton University Press, Princeton, New Jersey, 1994), pp. 20 and 102.

left brain function as a whole and give Woman advantageous qualities of non-hierarchical leadership.

HOW ANCIENT IS ANCIENT?

From this, it becomes more and more apparent why women in ancient societies held spiritual authority. However, considering that the term 'ancient' is most frequently used to imbue something with a degree of authority, one needs to question the generally held perception of what is ancient. 'Ancient Greece', for example is by far not really ancient but was already a patriarchal society. The foundation for the reversal of spiritual authority had been established in Greek mythology by way of a male motherhood. In Greece, Zeus "gave birth" to Athena through his forehead. He did this by swallowing Metis, the Goddess of Wisdom, while she was pregnant with Athena, and then having his forehead cleaved open into a vulva-shaped wound by an axe, from which womb Athena emerged. Fully clad in military armor. Could there be a clearer, more literal symbolization of male usurpation of woman's power?

Women in those times had already lost many of their former civic and economic rights, their property rights and their self-determination. Under the tight rule of marriage, both land and women fell under the sole ownership and control of man. But even into those times, the priestesses of the oracle of Delphi, the Sibyls, were so highly respected that they were consulted by rulers in matters of state, economics, politics and war. Their priestesshood and divination held spiritual authority and their counsel was recorded in the Sibylline Books, serving as a guide for those making the political decisions. We need to remember, however, that even this was a mere vestige of women's power from earlier times. The Greek hand that rocked the so-called 'cradle of civilization' was a male hand.

What was once the sacred site of the Goddess was usurped as the temple of a male god, Apollo. The Sibyl continued to prophesy, but credit was given Apollo, claiming that he possessed her spirit.

Finally, in 390 CE, the Byzantine emperor Theodosius destroyed the temple.

Max Dashu in her article "Priestesses, Power, And Politics" gives us a glimpse into how globally pervasive the usurpation of female spiritual authority has been, which conversely gives us a sense of how extensive woman's spiritual authority once was.

> *"A male takeover of women's rites and mysteries is described in oral histories from Australia, Melanesia, the Amazon basin, Tierra del Fuego, Kenya, Sierra Leone, and elsewhere. Encroachments on the sphere of priestesses are also attested in the pagan Mediterranean. The priests of Apollo took control of oracular shrines at Delphi and Didyma, interpreting the women's ecstatic utterances and forbidding women the right to consult the Pythias. Male hierophants also gradually consolidated their control of the Mysteries at Eleusis, where legal records show the Melissa priestess contested masculine trespasses on her traditional rights in the 4th century. And although ancient oral history says that Amazon queens founded the great temple of Artemis at Ephesus, women were later forbidden entry to its holy of holies, according to the Roman-era writer Artemidorus."* [24]

SELECTED JEWELS IN THE LINEAGE OF WOMAN

Though the inner stream of women's wisdom has been hidden, it has never been eradicated. Refreshing "springs" of women's wisdom have risen to visibility in patriarchal civilization such as these selected examples of women past and present who have acted from woman's natural spiritual authority. I call them Jewels in the Lineage of Woman. These Jewels, (Leymah Gbowee being one) which I prepared over a number of years for weekly presentation at The Goddess Temple of Orange County and The Southern Oregon Tem-

---

[24] http://www.suppressedhistories.net/articles/priestesses.html

ple of the Goddess,[25] honor women for their contribution to humanity whether as an artist, writer, scientist, activist, political leader, etc. Here, I am including some of the Jewels who acted from their innate spiritual authority on behalf of the human family. The common threads of self-referencing, female modes of power and Motherhood in action run through the lives and contributions of all these women.

(St.) Hildegard of Bingen (1098-1179)

Hildegard of Bingen (1098-1179) also known as "Sybil of the Rhine" was a known "first" in many fields. She was a Catholic nun, German abbess, mystic, writer, theologian, composer, artist, Sybil, and a healer known and quoted throughout Europe to this day. She was born the 10th child of a noble family and thus tithed, as was the custom, to the Catholic church.

Though she was very modest, Hildegard was deeply self-referenced in how she spoke, acted, wrote, taught and created her art. She even dared to chastise the princes and heads of state and the very Pope himself. And they 'took it' from her! This internal self-referencing began at age five with visions of luminous objects. She kept these visions to her self until adulthood when during the course of a serious illness she realized that the cure for the illness was to obey the promptings which had directed her to finally share these visions.

She founded convents and wrote plays, liturgies and hymns in praise of saints, virgins and Mother Mary. Through her images of the Virgin Mary, Sophia and of the Church itself as a female, she in essence revived the iconography of the Mother-Goddess while

---

[25] The GODDESS TEMPLE of Orange County, a women-only temple located in Irvine, California, was founded in 2002 by Ava Park. It was the inspiration for the 'co-ed' Southern Oregon Temple of the Goddess which was located in Grants Pass, Oregon (March 2007 to October 2010), founded an administered by the author and her husband Wolfgang Nebmaier.

working within the confines of the bastion of patriarchal male-dominated religion, the Catholic church.

The Hildegard Medicine, still taught and studied and used today, is based in her writings about natural history and about the healing powers and medicinal uses of plants, animals, trees and stones.

Hildegard's writings are also unique for their generally positive view of sexual relations and her description of pleasure from the point of view of a woman. They might also contain the first description of the female orgasm:

> *When a woman is making love with a man, a sense of heat in her brain, which brings with it sensual delight, communicates the taste of that delight during the act and summons forth the emission of the man's seed. And when the seed has fallen into its place, that vehement heat descending from her brain draws the seed to itself and holds it, and soon the woman's sexual organs contract, and all the parts that are ready to open up during the time of menstruation now close, in the same way as a strong man can hold something enclosed in his fist.*

Christine de Pisan (1364 - 1430)

Christine de Pisan was a French poet and arguably the first female author in Europe to make a living from being a writer. She had been left a widow at age twenty-five with heavy debt and three children and a mother and niece to support. Her writing countered the misogynist views which were so prevalent at the time that women were treated as second class citizens. Most men thought women should be restricted from inheriting of land and guild membership.

Much of her writing was autobiographical which was uncommon for writers of that time. She fought several lawsuits to recover the salary due her deceased husband.

How Ancient is Ancient?

Some feminists today consider her the originator of the feminist movement. She wrote from an inner referenced fountain of wisdom:

In *The Book of the City of Ladies* Christine de Pisan creates a city in which women are heralded for their past contributions to society. Three foremothers named Reason, Justice, and Rectitude offer counsel in how to overcome despair induced by societal misogyny.

In *The Treasure of the City of Ladies* de Pisan illuminates how women of all societal levels could counteract the growth of misogyny, particularly through the power of women's speech and everyday actions.

Olivia Durdin Robertson (b. 1917)

In 1976 Olivia Durdin Robertson co-founded the Fellowship of Isis, an international, multi-faith, multi-racial, and multi-cultural organization dedicated to honoring the religion of all the Goddesses and pantheons throughout the planet (the Gods are also venerated.) It is organized on a democratic basis, all members having equal privileges with membership now (2010) at 24,000 worldwide. Lady Olivia writes and presides as a priestess and oracle of the Goddess.

Marija Gimbutas (January 23, 1921 February 2, 1994)

was an archaeologist, professor, author and the founder of the genre of archaeomythology. She published nearly twenty books and over three hundred articles on European prehistory. She became a world-renowned expert on the Indo-European Bronze Age, Lithuanian folk art and the prehistory of the Balts and the Slavs.

Gimbutas considers her major contribution to be *"...the reconstruction of the meaning and functions of the Goddess"*. [26] By doing so she, like early 19th century female archaeologist Jane Ellen Harrison

---

[26] source: http://www.mavericksofthemind.com/gim-int.htm

and historian Matilda Joselyn Gage, challenged the established androcentric assumptions of the archaeological scholars.

She grew up in Lithuania where many of the Goddess-based pagan folk traditions had remained intact. Thus, she had a perspective through which she could interpret the symbols and purposes of the archaeological artifacts, a perspective her professional colleagues lacked. Her trailblazing research and interpretations had an incalculable impact on the modern Goddess spirituality movement and ultimately on the resurgence of woman's natural spiritual authority.

Of her own work, she said:

"Through an understanding of what the Goddess was, we can better understand nature and we can build our ideologies so that it will be easier for us to live."

Julia Ward Howe (May 27, 1819 – October 17, 1910)

Throughout her life, nineteenth century American writer, poet, reformer and lecturer, Julia Ward Howe worked for justice. She was an active advocate of abolition and, in 1861, she wrote The Battle Hymn of the Republic as an inspiration to Union soldiers fighting against slavery.

But in 1870 she was so grieved by the ravages of the American Civil War, that she called for a Mothers' Day with her Proclamation against war. This was no sentimentalized greeting card, no take mom to dinner day. This was a passionate admonition to *women* to put an end to war. Her Proclamation could not be more relevant to today.

MOTHERS' DAY PROCLAMATION

Arise, then, women of this day!
Arise all women who have hearts, whether your baptism be that of water or of fears!

How Ancient is Ancient?

Say firmly: "We will not have great questions decided by irrelevant agencies,

"Our husbands shall not come to us reeking with carnage, for caresses and applause.

"Our sons shall not be taken from us to unlearn all that we have been able to teach them of charity, mercy, and patience.

"We women of one country will be too tender of those of another country to allow our sons to be trained to injure theirs."

From the bosom of the devastated earth a voice goes up with our own. It says, "Disarm, Disarm!"

The sword of murder is not the balance of justice! Blood does not wipe out dishonor nor violence indicate possession.

As men have often forsaken the plow and the anvil at the summons of war, let women now leave all that may be left of home for a great and earnest day of counsel.

Let them meet first, as women, to bewail and commemorate the dead.

Let them then solemnly take counsel with each other as the means whereby the great human family can live in peace,

And each bearing after her own time the sacred impress, not of Caesar, but of God.

In the name of womanhood and of humanity, I earnestly ask that a general congress of women without limit of nationality may be appointed and held at some place deemed most convenient and at the earliest period consistent with its objects, to promote the alliance of the different nationalities, the amicable settlement of international questions, the great and general interests of peace.

Ada Aharoni

Professor Ada Aharoni is a Sociologist and a Peace Culture Researcher, writer, poet and lecturer. She has published twenty-seven books (she writes in Hebrew, English and French) which have been translated into several languages. In 1999 she founded and is President of IFLAC: The International Forum for the Literature and Culture of Peace.

Aharoni holds a truly radical vision for the power of the media to create peace. She points out that very little of our actual lives include homicide and murder, so why should our media be glutted with these topics? She is working to establish a World TV Satellite for the Culture of Peace which reflects our actual global and societal problems and offers solutions through the power of the arts, music, dance, literature, films and dialogues with writers and poets, including women, mothers and children, from both sides of the conflicts.

What makes her vision particularly potent, I believe, is to present coverage of politics and daily news about wars and conflicts, through the *eyes of mothers*, on *both sides* of the conflict.[27]

The Gulabi Gang

In India, Sampat Pal Devi, a member of the lowest "untouchable" caste, is the leader of a collective of women fighting injustice and restoring dignity to the untouchables. They wear pink saris and go after corrupt officials and boorish men with the power of shaming and when that does not work, as a last resort, with their traditional lahti sticks (long wooden staffs).

Sampat fights child marriage, she herself being forced to marry at age twelve. She lives in a hollowed out hut in the ground with her five children. One day, seeing a woman badly beaten by her husband she intervened whereupon the man turned to her and beat her also. The next day Sampat returned with several other women and her lahti stick and beat the man until he begged for mercy. From the beginning, Sampat understood the power of female soli-

---

[27] *http://www.iflac.com/* and
http://patrickjsammut.blogspot.com/2008/10/interview-with-ada-aharoni-from-israel.html

darity, she did not return to the abusive man alone, but with several women accompanying her.

The now forty-thousands strong women of India's northern Uttar Pradesh state's Banda area proudly call themselves the "gulabi gang" (pink gang). They protect women and children from beatings, oppose child marriage, and unearth corruption (such as in the distribution of grain to the poor), negotiate solutions to familial disputes. They fight corruption and bribery, they demand reluctant police officers to register cases for underprivileged people and have gained the grudging respect of officials.

The International Council of 13 Indigenous Grandmothers

Through a series of visions she received, Jyoti, (Jeneane Prevatt) founder of the Kayumari spiritual community in California felt guided to call together a Council of Indigenous Grandmothers from around the world. When she felt overwhelmed as to how would she find these Grandmothers, the inner wisdom spoke to her that the seed of everything is relations, to start there and the rest would unfold.

As a result, in 2004, she gathered a group of thirteen indigenous Grandmothers from around the globe, the fulfillment of a centuries old indigenous prophecy that, when humanity needed their guidance, a council of thirteen Grandmothers would form and offer their wisdom to humanity.[28] Their Mission Statement is:

WE, THE INTERNATIONAL COUNCIL OF THIRTEEN INDIGENOUS GRANDMOTHERS, represent a global alliance of prayer, education and healing for our Mother Earth, all Her inhabitants, all the children, and for the next seven generations to come. We are deeply concerned with the unprecedented destruction of our Mother Earth and the destruction of indigenous ways of life. We believe the teachings of our ancestors will

---

[28] Carol Schaefer, *Grandmothers Counsel the World: Women Elders Offer Their Vision for Our Planet*, (Trumpeter Books, Shambhala Publications, Inc., Boston, MA, 2006)

light our way through an uncertain future. We look to further our vision through the realization of projects that protect our diverse cultures, lands, medicines, language and ceremonial ways of prayer and through projects that educate and nurture our children.[29]

One example of where The Thirteen Indigenous Grandmothers are asserting woman's natural spiritual authority is their challenge to the Pope of the Catholic Church to rescind certain 15th century Papal bulls which, for centuries, have sanctioned massively devastating colonial policies of conquest, exploitation and genocide of indigenous peoples.

Luisah Teish

In an excerpt from *"Big Mamas and Golden Apples"*[30], Luisah Teish, writer, performer and ritual priestess and initiated elder in the Ifa/Orisha tradition, describes the women in the New Orleans community where she grew up in the 1950's. She recounts how in her community they believed that women's capacity to birth and nurture life from their body endowed them with special powers and abilities to engage with the forces of nature in ways that men generally could not. As a child, Teish observed how the women's prophecies and intuitions would materialize with uncanny accuracy. These women were midwives, herbalists, trance mediums and storytellers who trusted and depended on each other for healing illness, birthing babies, foreseeing natural disasters, tending to life passages around spiritual development and death. They were women adept at organizing the community, mediating family disputes and standing up against injustice. These women were drinking from the inner fountain of their lineage of women's wisdom, robustly living the reality of their natural spiritual authority.

Teish says they were known in her community as "the Mothers" (her capitalization) or the "big mamas".

---

[29] http://www.grandmotherscouncil.com
[30] *http://www.msmagazine.com/oct99/rituals.asp*

How Ancient is Ancient?

"Women like these exist in every culture on the globe. In some Native American cultures, they are called medicine women or cuaranderas; in European cultures, they are called witches. Among black folks that I know, we call them 'the Mothers.' They're the block mothers, the church mothers, the big mommas who hold our lives and communities together."

Yoga by Women Today

Among the modern surge of hardbelly-oriented yoga there is an undercurrent of women restoring the roots of female wisdom in yoga. The emphasis is on yoga as fluid, dynamic presence, energetic awareness in non-rigid posture and motion. It is natural that such yoga would manifest from Woman, for woman's body is cyclic, ever changing, fluctuating, like the rhythms of the moon. This is power, referenced in the body, reality itself and its non-conceptual, direct experience.

Some of these re-manifestations of the original yoga are *Continuum* as originated by Emilie Conrad, Dunya Dianne McPherson's *Moving Yoga*. *Feminine Unfolding* is what Angela Farmer calls a video of a deep exploration she does with a group of students. There is *La Madre Yoga* by Ruth Gould-Goodman, the *Yoga of Joy* by Yuan Miao and *The Tantric Dance of Feminine Power* a devotional, womb-sourced moving yoga originated by this author, Vajra Ma. And in an article, Vicki Noble, feminist author and originator of *Lunar Yoga* asks the rhetorical question: *"Did Women Invent The Ancient Art Of Yoga?"* Her research suggests that women had invented Yoga by the 7th millenium BCE and that the varied poses shown in early sculptures, frescoes, murals, and rock art are all expressions of an ancient and widespread female-centered communal practice of Yoga which was eventually codified into the formal schools that we recognize today.[31]

---

[31] http://www.yogahub.com/blog/women-and-yoga-by-vicki-noble/

Selected Jewels in the Lineage of Woman

Other Ground-Breaking Organizations and Publications

Women all around the world are raising their voices. Whether they call it that or not, they are reasserting Woman's Natural Spiritual Authority. To name but very few:

Urgent Message from Mother: Gather the Women, Save the World by Jean Shinoda Bolen[32]

Malalai Joya's *A Woman Among Warlords: The Extraordinary Story Of An Afghan Who Dared To Raise Her Voice*

Vicki Noble's *Shakti Woman*

The Women Waging Peace Network, part of The Institute for Inclusive Security

Gather the Women

Peace is Loud

Riane Eisler's Center for Partnership Studies

Barbara Marx Hubbard's Foundation for Conscious Evolution

Genevieve Vaughan's Gift Economy

Max Dashu's Suppressed Histories Archives

Dr. Heide Göttner-Abendroth's Hagia: International Academy for Modern Matriarchal Studies and Matriarchal Spirituality

Karen Tate's Voices of the Sacred Feminine, blog radio

Women on the Edge of Evolution

Z Budapest, founder of the Dianic Tradition

Code Pink

Marianne Williamson's Sleeping Giant

Ava Park's Queen Teachings, "When the Goddess got thrown out of religion, the Queen got thrown out of Woman"

---

[32] Bolen's book contains several examples of women effectively acting collectively in their natural spiritual authority including: the Madres de la Plaza de Mayo (Mothers of the Disappeared) in Argentina; six hundred Nigerian women successfully stopping local abuses by a major corporation; how some USA women achieved justice "outside the box" of costly litigation in instances of date rape and sexual harassment.

How Ancient is Ancient?

A few of the many Temples to the Goddess founded around the globe: Selena Fox's Circle Sanctuary; Covenant of the Goddess; the Reformed Congregation of the Goddess; Kathy Jones' Glastonbury Goddess Temple, England; Ava Park's Goddess Temple of Orange County in Irvine, California; Ruth Barrett and Falcon River's Temple of Diana, USA; The Temple of Goddess Spirituality Dedicated to Sekhmet, Nevada, founded by Genevieve Vaughan; Goddess Temple of Hungary; Loreon Vigne's Temple of Isis at Isis Oasis Sanctuary, central California.

THE GODDESS LIVES

The clues of woman's ancient spiritual authority persist into the modern world, they can be seen everywhere, once eyes and mind and heart are alert to them. My own Grandmother's glow-in-the-dark Mary statue is one such clue. The church grudgingly instituted Mariology in the 5th century CE as a means of keeping the people in the priestly folds of church authority by "giving them back" what they had never fully relinquished, their revered Goddess, albeit in submissive status, truncated in power. The people must have their Goddess! They had kept Her alive in their folk traditions and agricultural seasonal celebrations, still referred to as the "Old Religion", which originated from the centuries old spiritual view of the earth and cosmos as the sacred body of The Great Mother. Mother Mary with her holy child Jesus is herself a direct vestige of a much older sacred image, that of the ancient Egyptian mother goddess Isis and her divine son Horus. Indeed, the Holy Mother and Child is depicted in art around the globe and through the ages.

The Divine Mother lives today in Mother Earth (now even called by scientists by Her old Greek Goddess name, Gaia), in the Muse, in fairy godmothers, and demonized as the wicked step-mother, evil queen or wicked witch. She lives hidden in the Catholic saints: Goddess Brigid of Ireland is Saint Brigid, Tonatzin of South America is La Virgin de Guadalupe. In Santeria, the Goddess Yemaya is La Virgin de Regala, Oshun is Our Lady of Charity, and Oya is Saint Theresa. The Great Mother would have us be free and so She lives in Lady Liberty in countless classical western paintings and in the harbor of New York, holding aloft the ancient flame of Her enlightening power.

INDIGENOUS WISDOM

Since no one can completely erase reality, the legacy of the Great Mother has never been completely expunged and lives on not only in the survival of Mary and a revival of more ancient Goddess knowledge, but also in the indigenous wisdom carefully and consciously protected, preserved and passed down in various cultures and traditions around the world. While not all these lineages speak of a goddess, per se, they have maintained the wisdom of respect and right relationship with Woman and the Earth. These lineages have been maintained, at times consciously underground, and in some rare instances, due to a lack of contact with the outside world, they have been preserved fully intact, for the time when their teachings could surface again and help bring humanity back from the brink of disaster.

The Kogi of Colombia is one such intact lineage. They have stayed out of contact with the modern world. Their history and religion is passed down orally, their lives guided by the spiritual leaders or Shamans named "Mamas." They warn "younger brother" (modern 'man') that he is killing the Earth and we have two decades to change or face disaster. They came out of seclusion to deliver that message in 1992.

It is ironic that the very lineages which so-called civilized (that is, industrialized) nations have been deliberately and systematically trying to dominate and destroy are the ones which will help save us all, including those same colonizing 'civilized' countries. The wisdom teachings of these ancient lineages are emerging slowly but unstoppably into the global limelight at this crucial time. Their common denominator is to wake humanity up, remind us of our Source, call us back into right relationship with Earth and each other.

THE GREATER MOTHERHOOD OF THE COSMOS: THE GREAT COSMIC MOTHER

No word has a stronger connotation of multiple interrelatedness than the word "Matrix". It comes from the Latin 'mater', mother. No other image represents the relationship of power and responsibility more fundamentally and fully, more naturally than that of Mother and Child. No wonder Mother Mary persisted in spite of the doctrinal attempts to expunge Her. The image of Mother and Child speaks to our most primal level of survival as well as our most sublime aspirations and spiritual values. We need a mother.

Long before the image of a male god and long before the image of mother and child was subordinated to a male god (in both Western and Eastern religions) the image of mother and child stood preeminent as the image of the Divine. Earliest images of mother and child were not (virgin) mother and son, but mother and daughter. This makes supreme sense given the fact that early mythologies considered the Goddess parthenogenetic, self-born, and any progeny of a virgin, in the original sense of virgin as whole unto herself and belonging to no man, would be female, a daughter.

Woman is sustained by and channels the sustenance of The Great Cosmic Mother. This is the original spirituality of humanity.

THE ETERNAL CYCLE

The image of the *Double Goddess*,[33] (left side on next page) would allow the conjecture that the people who created it had some knowledge of the womb continuity, i.e. that the egg which

---

[33] Çatal Hüyük, Neolithic site in southern Anatolia (Turkey) with findings from between 8000 to 5000 BCE

becomes the child originally lived in the body of her mother's mother. We know today that every egg that a woman will ever have in her ovaries is fully formed while she is a fetus in her own mother's womb. Everyone was once in their grandmother's womb. Everyone is twice imbued with the vibration of a mother's heart, as depicted also in the

statue of Grandmother Ann, Mother Mary, and Jesus (right side). This is the physiological reality. It requires no mythology, no threat of withholding to be enforced or upheld.

Gradually, over centuries, the continuity of the queen and her daughter was supplanted by the queen and her son lover, then by the queen sharing the throne with her son lover as king, followed by the queen becoming the throne itself upon which the king ruled as supported and allegedly sanctioned by her, and finally, the king forced her off the throne and installed his rulership by might in full force. And to substantiate this claim to power, his "divine right of kings", he declared himself the emissary of a rather unyielding god or took on this role himself.

He ruled from the throne not side by side with She who creates life, but over all those "she's" (women) who give life, man over woman and other men, king over all, including Earth and her creatures and elements.

After all, "*then God said, Let us make man in our image, in our likeness, and let them rule over the fish of the sea and the birds of the air, over the livestock, over all the earth, and over all the creatures that move along the ground.*"[34]

The mother, whose reality, whose life giving power entitles her to authority, naturally, she and her biology are relegated to second fiddle; and where that is not enough to pound the reverence for life out of the people who still recognize her, she becomes the source of all evil.

Some (pseudo-) Christian fundamentalists go to any length to disseminate "findings" and interpretations "proving" this conviction. They refer to apparent linguistic facts claiming that the Hebrew word for "filthy" means "menstrual flux", and that the Hebrew word for "rags" means "clothing or garment" and conclude that "filthy rags" literally means garments that have been soiled by woman's menses blood. Some cite Leviticus (15:19-27) where it mentions that such menstrual blood defiles everything that it comes in contact with.

This type of view as our paradigm of authority, an authority which has lost its connection to the sacredness of woman's intrinsic power to create life and woman's intrinsic responsibility to that life, allowed that life to become commodified, to become cheap and dispensable in the world. Rampant child abuse, domestic violence, war, rape, genocide and femicide are the consequences.

THE POWER OF MOTHER AND CHILD AS SACRED SYMBOL

The depiction of mother and child is an ancient symbol, one that predates the modern patriarchal religions. We find it throughout

---

[34] Bible, "New International Version" (©1984)

The Goddess Lives

the tribal art of Africa, in the Egyptian Goddess Isis with her child Horus, in the European Neolithic images of anthropomorphized serpent mothers with serpent babies in their arms, and many other images in the same vein. It is an iconography of reverence to life.

In stark contrast, we have become inured to looking at a man being brutally murdered on a cross. This is the murder of a woman's child, her son. Have we become dulled to hundreds of thousands of murders of women's children today as well?

What would happen to war if one imagined God as female, as a great mother? Would a mother vanguard war? What happens to the relationship between justice and mercy? Would Justice be blind and unfeeling? What happens in our hearts, when we imagine coming to Mother, asking Mother for a boon, for help, for comfort?

How does the relationship to a Great Mother affect our relationship to the Earth, and to the food we produce? Would we imagine that She wants only some of her children to eat and the others to starve? Could we imagine the Mother's blessings on factory farms where mother sows are chained in metal cages called iron maidens, so small they cannot stand or turn around, but can only lie on their side, to nurse the babies who will soon be taken from them? Can we imagine Her blessing the factory farm where millions of cows, screaming and bawling in abject terror, are driven down the kill line to the killing floor, ankle deep in blood, to be hung up, fully conscious by one rear leg, their bones breaking from their weight, just so their heads can be lifted out of the blood as their throats are slit to satisfy the rigidly specific "kosher" requirements of "clean" slaughter? [35]

The list of horrors, kept from the public deliberately, goes on for every factory farmed animal species. When we see women holding their starving baby in their arms, what do we imagine a Great

---

[35] Contributed by Ava Park, founder of OCPA (Orange County People for Animals)

Mary, the Redeemer

Mother would do? What do we imagine She would feel? What do we imagine She would want us to feel? To *do*?

In a society devoted to a Great Mother, would we imagine that women rape one out of four men or demand that the men they rape cover their bodies and faces, head to toe, in heavy cloth, even in sweltering heat? Does the image of a Mother God inspire us to enslave little boys and sell them as sex toys for women around the world?

This, in reverse, is precisely what exists in the world today.

While for me, personally, the mother and child most certainly do not conjure up thoughts and feelings of war, violence and destruction, patriarchal religion names the biblical first woman Eve, meaning "mother of all living" then pronounces her the destroyer of the Garden of Eden and the bringer of death and suffering into the world. A Mother God, on the other hand, would She create a beautiful garden with luscious fruit and then forbid us to enjoy it? When we hungered for the knowledge in that fruit, would She call that evil and when we tasted that delicious fruit She had created, would She curse us for it?

And, finally, can there be any more urgent call for the Natural Spiritual Authority of Woman than these questions?

MARY, THE REDEEMER

The Madonna, mother and child is also revered in some patriarchal religions. Even the female lineage including the grandmother (Anne, mother of Mary) is depicted in a number of statues and paintings. But the church in Rome instituted Mary worship in the 4th century CE only because it had to in order to keep control of the common people who still turned to the Great Mother Goddess. And they still do today.

The image of the Mother Mary, the Mother Virgin, is a truncated one, of course, of a woman whose sexuality is lopped off into virginity, a woman alone among women, divided and separated from her sex, both by giving birth without sexual union and by her own "immaculate conception". Being the only woman who is herself conceived without original sin in *her* mother's womb as well, she is a woman who is not defiled by the blood of life. All other women remain the carriers of original sin in their wombs, remain the heirs of Eve's disobedience and the curse that came with it.

> *To the woman he said, "I will greatly increase your pains in childbearing; with pain you will give birth to children. Your desire will be for your husband, and he will rule over you."* Genesis 3:16[36]

This way, whether the Catholic church intends it this way or not, Mary becomes the redeemer of all women (in the above context). By associating with her, a woman uplifts herself from the (nearly) irreparable despair of original sin. It is likely that the devout Mary worshippers pervasive throughout much of early Christianity were not really aware of this regained power by women. But the formal church was definitely not done with their subjugation of Woman.

Inquisition and Rape

As a consequence, it promulgated the Inquisition, "The Burning Times", 400 years of the European Women's Holocaust, twenty generations of a war primarily against women in which (estimates vary widely) between 100,000 and 3 million women were declared "witches" and murdered. In some villages not a single female inhabitant remained.

The Malleus Malificarum (Hammer of the Witches) of 1487 was the Catholic Church's "authoritative" document for defining "witchcraft", trial procedures and punishment. Written by the two Dominican monks Kramer and Sprenger and officially sanctioned by the pope, it blatantly declared hatred and fear of Woman:

---

[36] Bible, "New International Version" (©1984)

Mary, the Redeemer

> *"What is woman but a foe to friendship, an unescapable punishment, a necessary evil, a natural temptation, a desirable calamity, a domestic danger, a delectable detriment, an evil nature, painted with fair colours!...When a woman thinks alone, she thinks evil."*[37]

And the following description of women illustrates in more detail the Great Reversal, that is, demonization of Woman's spiritual endowments of psychic sensitivity, linguistic intelligence and powers of the female shamanic group: Women are "*more credulous*" and "*naturally more impressionable, and more ready to receive the influence of a disembodied spirit*" and "*have slippery tongues, and are unable to conceal from their fellow-women those things which by evil arts they know...*"[38]

Making an evil of her spiritual sensibilities and female wisdom the Hammer says:

> *"For as regards intellect, or the understanding of spiritual things, they seem to be of a different nature from men; a fact which is vouched for by the logic of the authorities, backed by the various examples from the Scriptures."* (emphasis mine)

As the two priests explain why women were by nature evil and thus the instruments of Satan, they set the stage for enforcement of the women's holocaust on the grounds of the fundamental patriarchal reversal—the myth of male birth:

> *"But the natural reason is that she is more carnal than a man, as is clear from her many carnal abominations. And it should be noted that there was a defect in the formation of the first woman, since she was formed from a bent rib, that is, rib of the breast, which is bent as it*

---

[37] Heinrich Kramer and Jacob Sprenger, *Malleus Malificarum*, trans. by M. Summers (Arrow Books, London, 1971), pp. 114-115

[38] Ibid. p. 115

were in a contrary direction to a man. And since through this defect she is an imperfect animal, she always deceives..."[39]

The objective of that war on women was accomplished and is continuing.

But there is no thinking "that was then", nor that it was confined to history or to any one religion. Quite the contrary, that war rages on today in the form of domestic violence, rape, sex trafficking of children (particularly girls) and female genital mutilation. The victims number in the millions.

In "cultural" terms that war continues in Catholic priests' unchecked sexual abuse of children and in (pseudo-) Muslim 'honor' killings.

I will not grieve the reader here with details of the heart-rending horror of so-called "honor" killings which usually entail a brother killing his sister and sometimes the father and even the mother killing her own daughter, nor belabor rape as a terrorist weapon of war that is being committed with such brutality that those doctors who try to surgically restore women's bodies say the word "rape" is inadequate, it can only be called "sexual massacre". Suffice it to say that none of this could happen in a world that respects and reveres its own life-giver.

All rape, whether for genocide or not is an act of death. It dismembers the psyche of a woman, echoing the dismemberment of the Goddess. It suffocates a woman's flow of creativity, vitality and beauty. It is, ironically, also an attack on the source of the rapist's own life. Any woman's womb is every woman's womb.

---

[39] Ibid. p. 117

WHY IS BIRTH NOT A SACRAMENT
DE-SACRALIZING BIRTH

Women have been dismembered from their bodies at the most fundamental level, in the birth process.

We are laid down so that our vulva cannot open to the Earth and feel Her gravitational pull helping us. Then we are further disconnected from our birthing body with drugs and episiotomies while the doctor "delivers" the baby. When did women stop delivering their babies into the world? Why does a technician claim credit for life? More and more now, physicians induce birth to suit their weekend golf schedule or disrupt the vaginal experience by cutting the womb open and pulling the baby out in a Caesarian section. The modern hospital birth turns the womb over to a male-dominated industry whose roots lie in the extermination of the traditional medicine women and midwifes. It has, in fact, become a modern variation on the myth of male motherhood.

Birth, the first sacred experience in life has been de-sacralized. The natural waters of birth are judged insufficient. The child must be "born again" in the waters of baptism, cleansed of 'original sin', transferred, of course, from the origin of the child-woman's cursed body.

Male children in the Jewish and Muslim faiths are whisked away only a few days after birth to be subjected to circumcision, the blood shedding covenant that alters the natural body created by his mother, thus bonding him to his father god and the lineage of males.

Judy Chicago: Birth and Oppression

In the mid 70's the feminist visual artist Judy Chicago set out to create an art piece that used the birthing process as a metaphor for creation.

> *"My first ideas in developing imagery for the Birth Project involved using the birth process as a metaphor for creation... I went to the library to see what images of birth I could find. I was struck dumb when my re-*

search turned up almost none. It was obvious that birth was a universal human experience and one that is central to women's lives. Why were there no images?"[40]

She came to the realization that not only had the birth process been erased as a symbol of creation, but has been distorted by our societal (mis)values to oppress women:

> "...Exploring the subject of birth brought me face to face with the fundamental cause of women's oppression – as soon as one gives birth to a child, one is no longer free...It may be a high school girl being deprived of an education because she becomes pregnant; a woman on an airplane desperately trying to quiet a screaming child while everyone stares at her in disgust; a long married mother of three whose husband leaves her, her income thereby reduced to poverty level; or a highly gifted artist whose conflicts between self-fulfillment and her child's needs tear her apart with guilt. Whatever her situation, every woman who has a child is punished for having done the very thing which society tells her is her womanly goal."

Divide and Conquer

The institution framing that punishment is the structure of the nuclear family, placing the time, financial and energy demands on two people at best and even then, mostly on the woman. Women are separated into individual houses, a kind of dismemberment from the collective, left to struggle without an extended family, village or network of support to share the demands of parenting. Under this burden, a woman is left with little resources for herself. All suffer in this situation, the women, their partners and the children. Society suffers from the drain of vitality that would afford both better parenting and greater contributions to society as a whole by women. No one wins.

---

[40] Source for Judy Chicago's Artist Statement for The Birth Project: http://jwa.org/feminism/_html/JWA013.htm

A Time for Durga

Myths are truths which manifest on many levels. Most of the myths we are familiar with today reflect actual historical events played out and depicted on an over-arching scale. We have seen how many of these paint heroic pictures of rather despicable actions to justify or even deify the unnatural authoritarian might established by conquerors and oppressors.

On the other end of the mythological spectrum are myths like the one of the great Hindu Goddess Durga. It illustrates what happens when all else fails, when the paradigm of conquest and might fails and opposites have lost their vitality to transmute into each other. When the opposites are mired in dualistic opposition, only the Goddess, the Feminine Power can resolve the situation.

In the myth of Durga the gods and demons have been in prolonged battle, neither side gaining. The gods finally acknowledge the stalemate, that they cannot of themselves prevail. They combine their forces and call upon Durga, the Supreme Goddess. Durga appears and grants their request to defeat the demons. She goes to battle, serenely astride the lion, Her many arms, each equipped with a superlative weapon. After decimating the hordes of demons, she faces the final enemy, the leader of them all. Durga raises Her spear and thrusts it unerringly into the heart of the demon.

The myth of Durga is a myth of our time.

The resurgence of the Feminine Power will provide the power we need to pierce the demons of the modern era, spiritual ignorance, rapacious greed and violence. The desecration and ravaging of our Mother Source, Woman and Earth.

Durga's victory blow is a direct piercing of the heart. The Great Cosmic Mother asserts her supreme female power and authority, the only power that can pierce the heart of the demon.

This is the time for Durga in every Woman.

ABOUT VAJRA MA

Vajra Ma teaches outside the codification of established traditions and doctrines. She has designed and facilitated women's ritual since 1986 and has integrated Goddess knowledge and feminist spirituality with experiential body wisdom (the conscious awareness of subtle body energies) to forge Woman Mysteries of the Ancient Future Sisterhood™, a modern mystery school and Priestess lineage based in the devotional moving meditation she originated, The Tantric Dance of Feminine Power®.

Vajra Ma's **RED DOOR** priestess training in the lineage of the Ancient Future Sisterhood is an accelerated path of power into this unique synthesis of elements. Together with her associate and only authorized master teacher Nita Rubio, Vajra Ma offers an **APPRENTICESHIP PROGRAM** in The Tantric Dance of Feminine Power to those few women who are passionate and ready and have made the commitment to take on the rigorous training required to teach this lineage practice in its fullness, and with authorization.

Aside from her own books, the workbook for *The Tantric Dance of Feminine Power*, a nourishing mainstay for students and potential teachers of the dance and the present book, Vajra Ma is featured as contributor in *Daughters of the Goddess*, Wendy Griffin, ed. (Alta Mira, 1998) an anthology of women's spiritual work in America, in *Heart of the Sun*, Candace Kant, Anne Key, ed. (Goddess Ink, 2011) and her work has been the subject of scholarly papers presented at national conferences on religion.

About Vajra Ma

Vajra Ma holds ministerial credential through the Temple of Diana, USA, and has extensive background in dance studies and theatre arts. She teaches with warmth, humor and a bedrock compassion. She resides in the forests of Southern Oregon with her husband Wolfgang Nebmaier and their various dangerous pets.

For information on The Tantric Dance of Feminine Power go to Vajra Ma's website: *www.GreatGoddess.org*, and to Nita Rubio's website: *embodyshakti.com*

For outlines of suggested enactments and rituals for women: "Reclaiming the Natural Spiritual Authority of Woman", and for men: "Aligning with Mother Mind" please contact Vajra Ma at *VajraMa@GreatGoddess.org*.

SUGGESTED READING

Buddhist Goddesses of India by Miranda Shaw

Gyn/Ecology by Mary Daly

Kali's Odiyya, also *Medicine of Light* by Amarananda Bhairavan

Passionate Enlightenment by Miranda Shaw

Shakti Woman by Vicki Noble

Tantric Quest: An Encounter with Absolute Love by Daniel Odier

Tantric Yoga by David Frawley

The Chalice and the Blade by Riane Eisler

The Great Cosmic Mother by Barbara Mor and Monica Sjoo

The Cult of Divine Birth in Ancient Greece, also *Virgin Mother Goddesses of Antiquity* by Marguerite Rigoglioso

The Lady of the Beasts by Buffie Johnson

The Language of the Goddess by Marija Gimbutas

The Myth of the Goddess by Anne Baring and Jules Cashford

The Natural Superiority of Women by Ashley Montague

The Once and Future Goddess by Elinor Gadon

The Politics of Women's Spirituality Charlene Spretnak, ed.

The Spiral Dance by Starhawk

Dreaming The Dark by Starhawk

The Wise Wound by Penelope Shuttle and Peter Redgrove

Wheels of Life by Anodea Judith

Index

A

Aharoni, Ada 59
Ammachi 6
Ancient Future Sisterhood 10, 17
authority 11
  and authorship 6
  and humility 22
  and love 29
  and marriage 21
  and matrix 4
  and motherhood 6, 18
  and power 6
  and relationship 6
  and responsibility 6, 18
  and self-referencing 20, 21
  artificial 13, 21
  basis of Woman's definition of in natural 3
    spiritual authority 19
  double standard 21
  false 13
  natural 17

B

Bible 39, 69, 72
birth 5, 14, 15, 20, 35, 38, 48, 50, 62, 72. *See* myth of male birth; also male motherhood
  and cosmic power 1
  and oppression 75
  de-sacralized 75
  self 39
Buddha 22, 38
Burning Times, The 72

C

Catholic church 7
  and Hildegard of Bingen 55
  and Inquisition 73
  and Mary as Redeemer 72
  and the Thirteen Indigenous Grandmothers 62
  saints, formerly Goddesses 65
Chicago. Judy 75
Christine de Pisan 56
collective 27
  and raising children 27
  of women 60
  patriarchal consciousness 25
  power 30
  visioning 29
  wisdom 16
collective consciousness
  and myth 33
  male 25
  of women 16, 17, 25
Conrad, Emilie 63
consciousness
  and Mother Mind 6
  dream 46
  right brain 46
  through Woman's womb 44

D

Daly, Mary 2
Dashu, Max 45, 54
death 14, 15, 18, 31, 35, 42, 46, 62, 71
  and cycle of life and rebirth 47

Index

and menses 48
culture of 40
Eve as bringer of 71
female as bringer of 3, 36
Great Mother of Life and 42
demonization 2, 37
  of female body 26, 37
  of female body and flesh 7
  of female sexuality and
    authority 52
  of the Great Mother 2
  of woman 2, 42, 73
  of woman in fairy tales 65
Devi, Sampat Pal
  and the Gulabi Gang 60
dismemberment 7, 14, 26, 52, 76
  and giving birth 75
  and motherhood 7
  and rape 74
  in myth 7
  of the Goddess 41
Divine Mother 1, 65
  myth of 34
domination 13, 20
  male 34
  male, justified 36
Dunya, Dianne McPherson 63

E

essentialism 45
Eve 35, 71, 72
  and serpent 36
  as cognate of Yahweh 36
  as teacher 36

F

Farmer, Angela 63
female genital mutilation 74
Feminine
  as whole 40
feminine power 1, 25, 38, 63, 77

G

Garden of Eden 2, 35, 71
Gbowee, Leymah 23
Gbowee, Leymah 30
Gimbutas, Marija 57
Goddess 28
  and folk traditions of 58, 65
  and menses 51
  and parthenogenesis 67
  and Parthenogenesis 39
  of Laussel *See* Laussel
  of the Hunt 47
  roots of all religion 38
  spirituality movement 2, 28, 45, 58
  Temples of, today 65
Goddesses
  Aphrodite 42
  Asherah 38
  Athena, male birth of 53
  Brigid 65
  Cretan 38
  Cybele 38
  Durga 38, 77
  Gaia 65
  hidden as Catholic saints 65
  Ishtar 38
  Isis 38, 57, 65, 70
  Lilith 38
  Mary 39, 55
  Medusa 38
  Metis, of Wisdom 53
  Oshun 66
  Oya 66
  Parvati and Lakshmi 34
  Sekhmet, 38
  Sophia 55
  Tiamat 42
  Tonatzin 65
  Yemaya 65
god-hero 7
Gould-Goodman, Ruth 63

Index

Great Cosmic Mother 1, 67
Great Mother 2, 38, 42, 65, 66, 70
   and parthenogenesis 39
Great Reversal 2, 28, 73
Gulabi Gang 60

H

Hildegard of Bingen 55
honor killings 74
Howe, Julia Ward 58

I

Inquisition 72
International Council of Thirteen Indigenous Grandmothers *See* Thirteen Indigenous Grandmothers

J

Jesus 22, 38, 65, 68
Jewels in the Lineage of Woman 54
Johnson, Buffie
   and *Lady of the Beasts* 47
Jyoti, Jeneane Prevatt 61

L

Lascaux 43
Laussel, Goddess of
   icon of Woman's natural spiritual authority 43
Liberia 30
lineage
   female 71
   from within 11
   indigenous 66
   inner, of women's wisdom 62
   oldest spiritual on earth 1
   unbroken, of Woman 26
Lineage
   Jewels in the, of Woman 54
lioness 38
   and natural authority of motherhood 18
   and throne 38
   as epiphany of the Goddess 18

M

male motherhood 7, 15
   in Greek myth 53
Malleus Malificarum 73
Mary 55, 65, 68, 72
   as Redeemer 71
matricide 43
matrix 4, 10, 15, 20, 23, 24, 48, 67
menses 51, 69
   and shamanism 48
   origin of math, science, astronomy 44
menstrual hut 51
misogyny 2
moon lodge 51
mother and child 7, 65, 67
   as sacred symbol 70
Mother Creator 1
Mother Mind 5, 12
Mother-Goddess 55
motherhood 5, 6
   larger scope of 48
   unifying value 24
Mothers' Day Proclamation 58
myth 3
   and collective consciousness 33
   and dismemberment 7
   and male domination 33
   and spiritual authority 33
   and the Great Reversal 28
   Greek, of male birth 53

Index

of dismemberment and separation 41
of Durga 77
of male birth 35, 73
of male motherhood 7, 15, 35, 75
of the Goddess 39
patriarchal 41

N

natural
  definition of in naturl spiritual authority 17
natural spiritual authority and politics 32
Noble, Vicki 3, 63

P

parthenogenesis 39
  and virgin 67
peace 59
  and listening to women 16
  and media 60
  culture of 59
  is Loud 64
  key to planetary 8
  Women of Liberia, Mass Action for 23, 30
  Women Waging, Network 64
power *See also* feminine power
  authentic 21
  female Modes of 21
  power-with vs. power-over 6

Q

queen 68

R

rape 30, 69, 72, 74
  and video games 37
  on Democratic Republic of Congo 33
Rebienot, Grandmother Bernadette 16
relationship 13
reversal 15, 41. *See also* Great Reversal
Robertson, Olivia Durdin 57

S

self-referenced 20
separation 4, 12, 18
  and dismemberment of the Goddess 41
  and patriarchal myth 41
  artificial doctrine of physical and spiritual 4
  spiritual dogmas of and violence 29
serpent 36, 70
Shakti 1
  myth of 34
shaman
  woman as natural 48, 50
shame 23
  power of 33, 60
Shaw, Miranda
  and *Passionate Enlightenment* 52
solidarity
  and collective power and wisdom 26
  of women 32
  of women in India 61
  of women in Liberia 30
spiritual
  and the physical 4, 33

definition of in natural
   spiritual authority 18
dynamics of Woman's body 50
is political 7, 29, 31
lineage, oldest on earth 1
trumps political 32

T

tantric teachers
   women as 52
Teish, Luisah 62
Thirteen Indigenous
   Grandmothers 16, 61
throne
   and Goddess 38
   and lioness 38
   and usurpation of Woman's
     power 38
   male take-over 68
Tiamat
   and dismemberment 42
Tree of Knowledge 2
Tree of Life 2

V

violence 6, 14, 33, 34, 59, 69, 71, 74, 77

'justified' by myth 8
and video games 37
culture of 13
domestic 37
rationale for 29

W

war 34, 59
   against women 72
   and video games 37
   in Liberia 30
witch 72
witchcraft
   and Inquisition 73
woman
   definition of in natural
     spiritual authority 16
womb 9, 29, 45, 47
   and the hunt 47
   as author of spiritual life 50
   as physical creator 50
Women's Holocaust 72

Y

yoga
   by women 63
Yuan Miao 63

ALSO AVAILABLE FROM THIS AUTHOR:

The Tantric Dance of Feminine Power

Spiritual Knowledge through Sacred Sensual Movement

A Guide for Private Study, Group Work and Teachers

by
VAJRA MA

1996-2013 Vajra-Ma. All rights reserved.
ISBN: 978-1-60643-332-4
USD 24.50 (plus shipping)